STRANGE FROM HASTINGS

Volume Two

Wishing you all the best! But you won't be rid of me! love Tracy x

Best wishes for the future, Martin

All the best, Naya. x

Helena W...

By the same author

Strange Exits From Hastings (Volume 1)

Jack the Ripper at Last? The Life and Crimes of George Chapman

Women of Victorian Sussex: Their Lives, Occupations and Dealings with the Law

Mary Raleigh Richardson: the Suffragette Arsonist who Slashed the Rokeby Venus

Railwaywomen: Exploitation, Betrayal and Triumph in the Workplace

Notable Sussex Women: 580 Biographical Sketches

Typesetting and cover design by the author

First published in 2021
This imprint 2022

The Hastings Press
hastings.press@gmail.com
www.hastingspress.co.uk

ISBN 9781904109372
Printed in England by Mixam

LIFE IS INFINITELY Stranger than Anything which THE MIND OF MAN could INVENT

DEDICATION

This second volume of *Strange Exits* is dedicated to the readers of Volume One. Thank you for your enthusiasm, for your copious and generous praise, for your many lovely reviews, and for making Volume One the fastest-selling Hastings local history book of all time.

A NOTE ON IMPERIAL MEASUREMENTS

As a rule of thumb, an inch is about 2.5cm, a foot is 30cm, a yard is just under a metre, and a pound in weight is roughly half a kilo. The currency throughout the book is £ s d — pounds, shillings (s) and pence (d). There were twelve pence (12d) in a shilling (1s) and twenty shillings in a pound.

SOURCES

The main sources used were our local paper, the *Hastings & St Leonards Observer* (*HSLO*), and other papers on the British Newspaper Archive (BNA), Gale Historical Newspapers, *The Times* Archive, Ancestry.co.uk, FindMyPast, the Genealogist. com, NLS Maps, FamilySearch.org, newspapers.com, FreeBMD and the General Record Office (GRO).

ACKNOWLEDGEMENTS

I am grateful to Stephanie Hedger and David Green for their time and expertise in assisting with genealogical sleuthing and proof reading.
    I would like to thank the owners of websites about various aspects of Hastings history, including Lynda Russell (Hastings Pub History); Leon Pettit (hastingsfootballhistory.co.uk); 1066Online; richardpollard.co.uk (now, sadly, deleted); hastingspierarchive.org.uk; David Simkin (photohistory-sussex. co.uk).

Helena Wojtczak BSc (Hons) FRHistS
St Leonards-on-Sea, July 2022
hastings.press@gmail.com

CONTENTS

Fish Ponds Farm and environs on a 1741 map.

The fish ponds at Fish Ponds Farm in 1823.

1740

THE DEMON BARBER OF GEORGE STREET

FISH PONDS FARM

When the cook of Caterina Villa was bludgeoned to death in 1848 (see *Strange Exits* Volume One) T.B. Brett remarked that it was the first murder in Hastings for a century. The earlier crime, known as 'the Fish Ponds murder' was, he noted, 'barely remembered'. It's time to remedy that.

Lawrence Holliday was born in the Cotswolds in 1711. He moved to Hastings and set up as a barber at 68 George Street. In 1739, aged twenty-eight, he married Mary Smithers at St Clements church. The widow of a 'wigg-maker', she had three young children and it is almost certain that Holliday was the sole earner for his new family.

Among his wealthy customers was Thomas Avann, a sixty-eight-year-old yeoman farmer who lived at Fish Ponds in Fairlight. Mr Avann was a bachelor but his brother John, a married man with children, lived nearby.

Holliday allegedly became 'tempted by the reputed wealth' of Mr Avann and plotted to attack and rob him. At 5pm on Monday 8th September he went to Fish Ponds, contrived to be alone with his client — doubtless under the pretext of shaving him — then attacked the defenceless old gent. Mr Avann cried out, but his servants failed to respond for about half-an-hour, by which time the cowardly killer had found some valuables and dashed across the farm, his flight witnessed by several of his victim's unwitting labourers.

The lethal weapon was reputedly a hammer, although a knife may have been involved, judging by this lurid description in the *Morning Post*:

> A great Piece of the old Man's Skull was cut off, and the Blood which flew out of the Wound had sprinkled the Walls of the Room almost up to the Ceiling. He liv'd two or three Hours after, in extreme Misery, but never spoke.

On 11th September Mr Avann was buried at nearby St Andrew's church.

When Holliday was identified and apprehended, every effort was made to extract a confession, to no avail. Only after he was tried and convicted at the Sussex Assizes in Horsham in March 1741 did he grudgingly give a partial confession to the padre, admitting to the robbery but not to the murder. He, along with a few other miscreants, was sentenced to death but, whilst they were merely publicly hanged at East Grinstead, a special, far more gory fate awaited him.

The Daily Post.

FRIDAY, September 19, 1740.

From Haftings in Suffex we are inform'd, that at Fairlight, within a Mile of that Place, one Thomas Avan, an old Man, was murder'd in his own Houfe, at Five o'Clock in the Afternoon, on Monday fe'nnight, and robb'd of a confiderable Sum. He was alone, but his Servants fo near that they heard him cry out ; but not apprehending any thing uncommon, did not make Hafte enough to fave him ; the Fact being committed and the Murderer gone in about half an Hour ; tho' he was feen by feveral Perfons at work in the Fields, who either were not time enough inform'd of his Villainy, or had not Prefence of Mind enough to feize him. A great Piece of the old Man's Skull was cut off, and the Blood which flew out of the Wound had fprinkled the Walls of the Room almoft up to the Ceiling. He liv'd two or three Hours after, in extreme Mifery, but never fpoke. A Fellow is fince taken up, and committed to Battle Goal, on Sufpicion of being the Murderer.

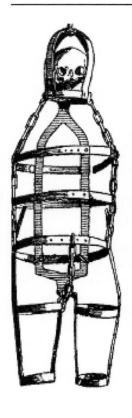

Extract of a Letter from Haftings, April 2, 1741.

' Lawrence Holliday, late a Barber in this Town, being at the laft Affizes held for the County of Suffex, convicted of the robbing and murdering Thomas Avann, a wealthy Farmer within a Mile of this Place, was Yefterday, (purfuant to his Sentence,) executed at Farleight Down, near which the Facts were committed, and afterwards hang'd in Chains there. Notwithftanding there was a prodigious Snow and Rain for many Hours, yet Multitudes of People from all Parts of the Country came to fee the Execution ; and the High Sheriff (living in the Neighbourhood) was alfo prefent, with his Officers and Attendants. The Prifoner was efcorted to Execution by a Party of Dragoons. All poffible Endeavours were ufed to obtain a full Confeffion of the Crimes for which he fuffer'd, but without the defir'd Effect ; though after his Conviction, and before he left Horfham, he admitted that he had but his Deferts ; and the Night before his Execution he made fomething of a Confeffion to the Rev. Mr. Brooke, wherein he acknowledg'd the Robbery, but not the Murder, though this was made in fuch an inconfiftent Manner, that by no Means became the Sincerity which a Perfon in his Circumftances ought to have had.

London *Evening Post* 4 April 1741.
A gibbet cage; this one has iron bands as well as chains.

Firstly, he was clapped in irons, then a party of dragoons escorted him back to Hastings, and then, on April Fool's Day, he was taken to Fairlight Down and publicly hanged.

> Notwithstanding there was a prodigious Snow and Rain for many Hours, yet Multitudes of People from all Parts of the Country came to see the Execution; and the High Sheriff (living in the Neighbourhood) was also present, with his Officers and Attendants.

Afterwards Holliday was gibbeted: his corpse was encased in a made-to-measure cage of tightly fitting chains and suspended from a post over 20ft high. It remained on public display as it gradually rotted, putrefied and fell to pieces, all the while doing service as a grisly and rather macabre tourist attraction. Sarah Tarlow describes gibbeting as 'the spectacular bodily punishment par excellence...It is pure theatre'. Thousands would attend to see an execution and gibbeting, many travelling considerable distances. The event was anticipated with relish, enjoyed as a rowdy and carnivalesque day out — complete with picnic — and reminisced about for decades.

The purpose of gibbeting was to shame and humiliate the criminal as well as to act as a deterrent to other would-be offenders. The post was always erected close to the scene of the crime, in a conspicuous spot, preferably on raised ground, and near a well-used road. The location chosen for Holliday's gibbet was near Fairlight Mill (now the site of North's Seat) and the many users of Mill Lane would never forget the foul stench of the corpse and the eerie creak of its chains as it swung gently in the breeze.

With an average of one a year, Sussex was second only to London in the frequency of gibbeting in the 1740s (neighbouring Hampshire had only one in the entire decade). From 1751 the corpses of murderers were by law either gibbeted or used for medical research (female bodies, being rarer, were always consigned to the latter fate, and were 'dissected and anatomised').

Over the decades gibbeting declined until it was abolished by statute in 1834. Public hangings, however, continued until 1868.

Holliday's unfortunate spouse, the twice-widowed Mary, must have been shocked by her husband's murderous actions as well as pained by his gruesome end. She married for the third time in 1746 and had two more children.

According to Manwaring Baines, upon Holliday's execution his house at 68 George Street became the property of Hastings Corporation, which sold it to William King in 1751. It is now the Clockwork Crow, two doors away from a shop called Flibberti*gibbet*(!)

References: *Daily Post* 19 September 1740; *Evening Post* 4 April 1741; John Manwaring Baines (1955) *Historic Hastings*; S. Tarlow (2015) *The Golden and Ghoulish Age of the Gibbet in Britain.*

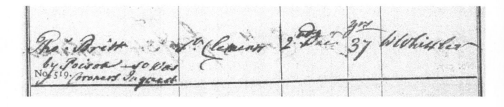

MARRIAGES solemnized in the Parish of *St Clements — Hastings*
in the County of *Sussex* in the Year 18*15*

Thomas Britt — (Bachelor) of *this* Parish

and *Sarah Ranger — (Spinster)* of *this* Parish

were married in this *Church* by *Banns* with Consent of

this *fifth* Day of

Dec in the Year One thousand eight hundred and *fifteen*

By me *Webster Whistler (Rector)*

This Marriage was solemnized between us { *Thos. Britt*
Sarah Ranger

In the Presence of { *Elizabeth Ranger — Ann Gray* + *her mark*
John Ranger

No. 79.

The Rev Whistler's entry in the All Saints' marriage register when Thomas 'Britt' married Sarah Ranger 5th December 1815. Unusually, both bride and groom could sign their names.

The entry of the burial of Thomas 'Britt' in the All Saints' burial register, 2nd December 1826.

Thos. Britt — *St Clement* 2 *Dec* 37 *W Whistler*
by Poison — so was
No. *519.* *Coroners Inquest*

1826

The Fishing Boat Mystery

Thomas Brett was born in Hastings in 1788. After being apprenticed to his father, a blacksmith, in due course he ran his own successful smithy in George Street. He married Sarah Ranger in 1815 and the couple produced five children, losing one in infancy — a common occurrence at that time. Thomas's business thrived and by 1826 he had saved enough cash to buy a share in a fishing boat. Drawn increasingly to the idea of life as a fisherman, he began to absent himself from home to spend time on the boat, even sleeping in it sometimes.

On Sunday 19th November 1826 Thomas was spotted early in the morning perched on a capstan. It turned out to be the last time he was seen alive. Later his eldest son Thomas, aged ten, found him lying dead in his boat on the shingle opposite the Cutter Inn. He was only thirty-seven and physically fit and strong from working for twenty years as a blacksmith.

Doctors Chapman and Ranking conducted a post mortem and their findings were presented to the coroner and his inquest jury. Thomas Brett was well known as a steady, reliable family man, and the entire town was shocked when it was revealed that arsenic had been found in his remains. 'Diligent search has been made at the various druggist's shops to ascertain if any poison had lately been vended, but without effect', explained the *Sussex Advertiser,* 'and the affair at present remains involved in the greatest mystery'. When he was buried at St Clements on 2nd December the rector, Webster Whistler, added the words: 'by Poison, so was Coroner's Inquest' beneath his name in the parish register.

Thomas Brett had no obvious reason to kill himself and left no note stating his intention to do so. He had a good life, or so it seemed. He was healthy, successful and financially secure; he had a loving family which depended upon him, and his wife was heavily pregnant with their seventh child. The baby was born a few weeks later but did not survive infancy.

Sarah Brett was lucky compared with most widows: she did not struggle for too long to support her family on her meagre earnings as a laundry ironer. In 1829, aged thirty-seven (and, for the record, two months pregnant) she married twenty-eight-year-old bachelor and blacksmith William Woolgar. He later became a builder, and was able to teach his stepsons some useful skills.

Sarah's eldest child, Thomas Brandon Brett, grew up to be the most remarkable man Hastings has ever produced. Born in George Street on 30th May 1816, the loss of his father forced him to grow up quickly. At the age of ten he was helping his mother with the housework and caring for his younger siblings so she could go out to work.

From humble beginnings as a draper's errand boy, T.B. Brett blossomed into a polymath whose multifarious occupations and hobbies encompassed baker, tailor, postmaster, school founder and master, musician, composer and leader of a brass band, dancing-master, co-founder of a mechanics' institute, stationer, journalist and printer. He founded two local newspapers: the monthly *Hastings & St Leonards Penny Press* and, in 1855, the weekly *Hastings & St Leonards Gazette*, which he published for forty years.

His 'Manuscript History of Hastings and St Leonards', and his historico-biographies of many interesting local people make for fascinating reading. East Sussex Libraries scanned each page, to preserve them, and to make them more accessible to the public. These scans have been transcribed into searchable text by a team of volunteer typists led by local historian Roy Penfold.

After an extraordinarily productive life spanning almost the whole of the nineteenth century, T.B. Brett died at the age of ninety.

Thomas Brandon Brett 1816-1906

1832

Mud Jack's Wife

George Street

In his manuscript histories, T.B. Brett twice quoted a poem composed by 'The Postman'[1] about a murder that supposedly occurred on 13th April 1832:

> In a timber-yard of Ball's — now Albion Mews —
> One 'Mud Jack's' wife some brute did badly use;
> Whose lifeless form, as seen by morning light
> Had undergone ill-treatment in the night.
> A fallen creature was that 'Mud Jack's' wife,
> Yet God alone should take away the life.

Brett later stated that a murder in 1848[2] was the first in Hastings for a century. Clearly, he did not count this one, suggesting that the verse was based on folklore, or a snippet from a ballad or sea shanty. However, Brett had cited a specific date, and, what is more, the second time he quoted the poem he added that he had seen 'the body of the poor woman as it lay in the van'.

This created a paradox. If the murder was real, why did Brett not report the details (as was his lifelong habit), or at the very least give the victim's name and reveal whether the culprit was caught? And why did he disregard it when citing local murders between 1740 and 1848? I resolved to discover the answer to this intriguing puzzle!

Hastings had no newspaper prior to the founding of the *Hastings & St Leonards News* in 1848,[3] but the *Sussex Advertiser* began in 1822 and is online. Having no name for the victim, I typed in 'Mud Jack's wife' and searched within the year 1832. Of course I expected to find nothing, because a newspaper would use the victim's real name. I was therefore astonished to read this sentence in the Hastings section of the edition of Monday 23rd April 1832:

> A poor woman, the wife of a man called *Mud Jack*, was found dead in a van, in a wheelwright's yard on Friday.

This sentence, though brief, felt monumental because it confirmed beyond any doubt that the poem was about a real incident.

1. 'The Postman' was actually Brett himself.
2. 'The Cook of Caterina Villa' in *Strange Exits From Hastings* Volume One.
3. There was one called the *Iris*, which started in 1830, but it folded in 1831 and is not online.

The first mention of the murder was in this handwritten memoir of T.B. Brett, published in Vol 1, Chapter VIII (H) of his manuscript histories. It reads:

> **On the 13th of April the
> wife of a man nick-named
> "Mud Jack" was found dead
> in under suspicions of foul
> play, in wheeler Ball's yard.
> Thus described by "The
> Postman"**

The poem by 'The Postman', reproduced on page 13, then follows. *Below:* the confirmation, *Sussex Advertiser* 23rd April 1832.

> Good Friday was observed here with the highest degree of decorum. The shops were closed, and divine service performed in the various churches and chapels.
>
> A poor woman, the wife of a man called *Mud Jack*, was found dead in a van, in a wheelwright's yard on Friday.

The murder was not deemed sufficiently important to lead the Hastings column. The top story was that the bells of St Clements and All Saints' had 'rung a merry peal' to welcome the new rector. Second place went to a report that 'Good Friday was observed here with the highest degree of decorum'. Last of all came the brief news item about poor 'Mrs Mud Jack'. The item was repeated verbatim in the *Maidstone Journal*, *Baldwin's London Weekly Journal* and the *Public Ledger*, but none added any additional details.

Confirmation that the murder was real made Brett's statements paradoxical. He was fifteen when he saw the corpse; surely such a shocking sight, and, indeed, having a murder right there in his 'patch' — in the very street in which he was born, and where he was up and down all day for his job as an errand boy — would stick in his mind forever.

I challenged myself to identify the victim from the scanty details available. A 'fallen' woman was perhaps a prostitute. The nickname 'Jack' suggests her husband was called John, unfortunately the commonest male name. Worse, it was also used to mean any unknown man (e.g. spring-heeled Jack, Jack Sprat, Jack-in-the-box, Jack Frost, Jack-in-the-green, Jack o'Lantern, Jack-of-all-trades, Jack the Ripper). 'Mud Jack' might be a crossing sweeper, a market gardener, or a man who emptied privies. All three lines of enquiry led nowhere.

The newspaper report corrected Brett's date for the incident from 13th to 20th April 1832. The civil registration of deaths did not begin until 1837, but some parish burial registers are online. I could search for females interred in Hastings after 20th April 1832, but without a surname how could I know which one was 'Mrs Mud'? The likelihood of being able to give Mrs Mud Jack her real name was evaporating by the minute.

For every murder there must be a coroner's inquest, and I must find a report of it, because I had nothing else to go on. There was nothing about the murder in the subsequent *Sussex Advertiser* but in the 7th May edition, halfway down page 4, I found mention of the inquest:

> An inquisition was holden on view of the body of the poor woman, who in a former paper we stated to have been found dead in a van, in a wheelwright's yard in this place, when the Jury returned the following verdict — '*Found strangled by some person or persons unknown*'.

The victim remained nameless and the murder was again relegated to the final story in the Hastings column. Nevertheless it gave the cause of death and revealed that, by the day of the inquest, nobody had been charged.

I wondered if another Sussex paper had revealed the victim's name. A keyword search of the *Brighton Guardian* returned no hits, so I painstakingly read every column of the 25th April edition from top to bottom. Although it comprised only four pages, they were printed on broadsheet, the largest size of newspaper page, onto which was crammed thousands of words printed in a tiny font.

Ball's yard is behind the building visible in the gap, to the left of the Albion Hotel.

Contemporary view of the West Hill Arcade, formerly Albion Mews, which in 1832 was the yard of wheelwright James Ball.

Just as my task was beginning to feel like a wild goose chase and my enthusiasm started to ebb away, my dogged determination at last paid off. Suddenly there it was, on page 3, beneath an article listing the arrivals and departures of the upper classes to the new town of St Leonards, and after a paragraph extolling 'The elegant science of archery' and 'the fair Toxophilites, inspired doubtless by Cupid'. At first glance the report of the inquest looked a good length and so, in anticipation of a riveting read, I settled down, ready to devour every word and detail.

I was deeply disappointed. Two-thirds of the article's thirty-one lines was used up on explaining how annoyed some jury members were that two local surgeons had opened the corpse before they had a chance to examine it exactly as found. The reporter then added his tuppence-worth on the matter, leaving a mere ten-and-a-half lines to tell the story of the murder, the investigation, the inquest and the verdict. The only salient facts revealed were:

~ Her name was Alderidge but she was known as 'Mad Jack's Wife'. *Mad*, not *Mud*!

~ She was 'a notoriously bad character' and 'exceedingly addicted to drink'.

~ The timber yard was that of Mr Bull, the wheelwright.

~ The body was carried to St Clements poor-house (42 George Street now covers the site) where, on Easter Saturday, the post mortem was conducted.

~ A number of people were questioned, but nobody had yet been charged.

The report was followed by the announcement that Thomas Emary was building a new hotel, to be called The Albion. The back of it was directly opposite the murder scene, and the wheelwright's yard would soon become its mews.

From other sources I found that the wheelwright was James *Ball*, not *Bull*.[4] The coroner was J.G. Shorter[5] and the surgeons who conducted the post mortem — and enraged the jury — were William Ross Chapman of 49 High Street and Robert Ranking of 79 High Street.[6]

On the day of the inquest, 24th April, the murderer was still at large. Although Hastings was the first town in Sussex to have a police force, it was not founded until 1836. Before then crime prevention, detection and investigation were in the hands of illiterate watchmen, busy-body beadles, a handful of untrained sworn constables, a bench of wealthy landowners appointed as

4. Ball was nicknamed 'Old Wheeler'. His wife died in 1838, leaving him with eleven children to raise, and by 1842 he was bankrupt.
5. John Goldsworthy Shorter (1804–1857) town clerk and coroner, committed suicide by shooting himself in the head. His own deputy conducted the inquest.
6. Ranking was a magistrate, jurat and Freeman of Hastings, and mayor in 1833 and 1836.

magistrates, and a solicitor who acted as coroner. It is almost certain that none had any experience of handling a murder enquiry.

Discovering the victim's real surname was a massive breakthrough and would lead to more facts being uncovered. I asked family history sleuth Stephanie Hedger to join me in the search; she tackled the SFHG[7] burials database whilst I scoured the St Clements parish register on FamilySearch.com. We both found her: Martha Aldridge, aged thirty-four, was buried at All Saints' on 24th April.

Having established her name and age we searched the baptisms database for her offspring. We found two daughters: Martha and Mary Ann, christened on 8th December 1820 and 22nd August 1828. Their father was a labourer called John. So, 'Jack' was John, after all. From this we swiftly found their marriage, solemnised at St Clements church on 14th October, 1819 by William Coghlan, a twenty-three-year-old curate.[8] In the register, he spelled John's surname 'Haldridge', and that is how John signed it, too. However, the children were baptised and Martha was buried without the 'H'.

The St Clements parish register revealed that Martha was also christened there, on 16th February 1798, that her parents were John and Mary Edwards, and that her first child Martha had died aged fifteen months.

A search for 'John Aldridge' in the Sussex papers between 1820 and 1850 drew a blank, so on a whim I tried 'Mad Jack'. To my surprise I found this short piece in the Hastings column of the *Sussex Advertiser* on 21st January 1828:

> A man, well known under the cognomen of Mad Jack was found guilty of an assault on his wife's mother, and sentenced to two months' imprisonment and hard labour in Lewes House of Correction.

In the 1820s it was seen as cowardly for a man to strike a member of the 'weaker sex', and to attack his own mother-in-law was shameful. If John was known as 'Mad' Jack, what earned him the nickname? Was he a harmless eccentric, like his contemporary 'Mad Jack' Fuller,[9] or was he literally mad?

John Aldridge was emerging from the shadows as someone who would physically attack a woman, and who was possibly mentally ill. His wife was strangled to death, the suspect escaped unseen, nobody confessed, and after she died there is no record of John in Hastings. Mary Ann (who was three when her mother was killed) appears in the 1841 census aged twelve, living with her mother's brother (a fisherman) in Vines Row, a down-at-heel backstreet in the Old Town.[10] Wherever her father went, he did not take her with him.

7. The Sussex Family History Group, www.sfhg.org.uk
8. Coghlan left in 1824 when the Duke of York appointed him to the position of Domestic Chaplain.
9. John Fuller (1757–1834), squire of nearby Brightling, High Sheriff of Sussex, MP for Sussex, a generous philanthropist, patron of the arts and sciences, builder of follies and noted eccentric.
10. After 1841 Mary Ann becomes impossible to pinpoint because many others had the same name.

Nobody was ever charged with killing Martha. Considering that almost every female murder victim was killed by her male partner, John is the prime suspect. Maybe rumours began to spread; perhaps whispers, stares and sideways glances pricked his conscience; Martha's parents may even have openly accused him, especially if he were the same Mad Jack who attacked his mother-in-law.

John has proved impossible to track down. There is no death record for him in Hastings, and no trace of a 'John Haldridge' anywhere. Conversely 'John Aldridge' gains hundreds of hits in genealogical records, criminal registers and newspaper archives, and it is impossible to say which — if any — were him.[11] There were Aldridges in Hastings in the decades before John was born; indeed, a William of that name, the captain of a smuggling boat, was shot dead by revenue officers in 1806 and buried in All Saints' churchyard.

When John left Hastings he could have gone anywhere, even abroad. I discovered an entry in a ship's manifest which reveals that, on 4th May 1832 — just two weeks after the murder — a man called John Aldridge sailed from Plymouth to New South Wales in a vessel called *Brothers*. After a journey of nearly four months he arrived on 25th August. He had no wife or children with him, gave his occupation as 'servant', and his passage was paid by the government under the assisted migration scheme.[12]

At the time, perpetrators of serious crimes were often sentenced to be transported. Could John, eaten up with guilt, have 'sentenced' himself to a similar punishment? Or did he simply want to get as far away from Hastings as possible, so that if the inquest was reopened, he could never be found? An Australian newspaper reported in 1863 that a John Aldridge had been charged with threatening to kill his wife.[13] John would have been about sixty-five. Could it have been him?

Mud Jack's wife is no longer nameless. She was Martha Aldridge, daughter of John and Mary Edwards, born in early 1798, died 20th April 1832, wife of John and mother of Mary Ann. The latter is likely to have married and had children, and so Martha may well have descendents who are alive today.

Brett's paradox remains unsolved. We will probably never find out why, despite having seen the corpse with his own eyes, he claimed there was no murder in Hastings between 1720 and 1848.

T.B. Brett's poem about Martha's death, which was until recently buried within a huge pile of obscure and unpublished personal reminiscences, filed away in a back room of a reference library, is now easily available to anyone, anywhere in the world, because of Roy Penfold and his monumental, heroic project to digitalise Brett's reminiscences.[14]

---

11. For example in the 1841 census there are 51 John Aldridges born between 1790 and 1800.
12. Between 1815 and 1840, assisted migration schemes helped 58,000 people to move to Australia to introduce some non-convicts into the country.
13. *The Age* 25 July 1863, via www.trove.na.gov.au
14. See http://historymap.info/Category:Manuscript_Histories

Martha Aldridge: documents from St Clements parish church registers.

The marriage of Martha and John in 1819 and (detail, enlarged) the bride and groom's signatures on the register. As almost all labouring people were illiterate, it is interesting that both were able to sign their names, though John's signature looks more like Halbridge than Haldridge. They both wrote with an idiosyncratic flourish; John's J and H were particularly ornate, whilst Martha displayed an interestng back curl on her D's.

The baptismal entries of Martha's two daughters in 1820 and 1828.

| BURIALS in the Parish of *St Clement's, Hastings* | | | | |
| in the County of *Sussex* | | | in the Year 18*32* | |
Name.	Abode.	When buried.	Age.	By whom the Ceremony was performed.
Martha Aldridge No. 778.	*St Clements*	*April* *24*	*34*	*F. Lipscomb* *Minister*

The record of Martha's burial.

The site of the murder as it is today. The buildings are the remains of Albion Mews.

The photo of the back of the Swan and a sketch of the front. *Russell.*

A postilion.

THE PITCHFORKED POSTILION

The Clase, Claiss, Claisse, Clace or Claice (spellings varied) family is descended from French nobility. In the 1300s a Claisse was knighted by Charles V for bravery at the Battle of Mountfort. His grandson became a count, and a descendant of his was created Duc de Bearn by Charles IX. During the French Revolution the family's estates were confiscated and their owner executed. The duc's son became a silk weaver, and his son fled to England and settled in Winchelsea; later, some descendents moved to Guestling.[1] In England the family was an ordinary one of the labouring classes, their name the sole remnant of their noble heritage.

John Clase (the spelling favoured by clergymen filling in their parish registers) was born in Winchelsea in 1799 and married Maria Merricks at Guestling in 1821. As the marriage record shows, they were both illiterate. By the age of thirty-four John had fathered six children and another was on the way. Described as 'a young man of excellent character...highly respected in the town', he worked at the Swan Hotel as a post boy or postilion (someone who rode on the left-hand horse of the pair that drew a post-chaise).

> As a posting house, the Swan provided a complete range of transport services. You could have your horse baited (fed and watered) or you could hire a horse to ride or to use with your own carriage. By the mid-18th century the Swan had acquired several coach houses, stables with granaries, a harness room and a brew house.[2]

One day Clase was in the stable tending to the horses when a colleague, twenty-four-year-old Edmund Walker, joined him and 'some joking commenced' between them. 'Unhappily the expressions which fell from [Clase] aroused the ill-feeling of [Walker], who suddenly seized a stable fork and plunged one of the prongs into the body of poor Clase. The wretch repeated his blows, and forced the fork through the lips, and inflicted two other wounds in the face, and then left the poor fellow weltering in his blood'. Walker was 'pursued and taken'.

After being questioned by magistrates, Walker was held in Hastings Gaol pending the outcome of his murderous attack. John Clase lay 'in a most dangerous state, and but faint hopes are entertained of his recovery.' Luckily for Walker, he survived, so when he was tried at the Hastings Sessions on 11th January 1835 it was only for assault, for which he was sentenced to six months' imprisonment.

1. Paraphrased from the writings of Anthony Crespigny, Heraldry College, Doctors Commons. 1880.
2. Lynda Russell, hastingspubhistory.com

John Clase set out on the long road to recovery, without painkillers or antibiotics. His wife bore a seventh child, and he managed to give her one last baby before he expired in 1840. The cause of death was 'decline', which meant his health had gradually deteriorated as a consequence of the assault. He was just forty-one. If any attempt was made to re-open the case and charge Walker with manslaughter, there is no record of it.

Poor Mrs Clase was left to raise eight children on her meagre earnings as a laundress.

Having served his sentence, Edmund Walker enjoyed a long life, working as a post boy, a coachman and, in later life, as a stable-hand. He sired six children and ended his days living in Shepherd Street, St Leonards.

References: *The Globe* 6 November 1834; *London Daily News* 22 April 1903.

The original lockup was in Courthouse Street. This fell into disrepair and was replaced in 1820 with a gaol a little further north (pictured). This was enlarged in 1832 and another storey was added. It is easy to establish the location because the former George pub (later the King's Head, now closed) is on the left of the picture, and the theatre on the right became a chapel, which was replaced by the Bourne Hall, which was recently converted into flats.

1826 & 1836

Pugilistic Quartet

All Saints' Church & Wellington Square

On 16th November 1826 a 'pugilistic rencontre' occurred between John Sinden, a teenage butcher, and George Foster, a twenty-four-year-old labourer who had married just four days earlier. They met in a field by the fence of All Saints' parish garden for the purposes of a bare knuckle fight, Henry French and Christopher Fielder acting as their seconds.

After shaking hands the men 'set to, and fought with great perseverence'. The younger man easily got the better of Foster, who received many severe blows to his head. The others carried him home and put him to bed. The next morning his newly wedded bride 'found him a corpse by her side'. The coroner's jury returned a verdict of manslaughter against Sinden, and aiding and abetting against the other two. All three were locked in Horsham Gaol to await trial. At the spring assizes each man was fined £1 and released.

* * *

In the 1830s lime was in great demand in Hastings as a building material. It was created by heating chalk (which arrived by ship from Eastbourne) in kilns. This was thirsty work, and the kiln labourers frequented a number of beershops. One day in 1836, George Tapsell, the nineteen-year-old son of an ostler, and David Cousens, forty-one, a bricklayer, husband and father of eight (the youngest a babe in arms) enjoyed a few refreshing pints of ale in the Plasterer's Arms. They became embroiled in a drunken quarrel, and the older man challenged the younger, in time honoured fashion, to 'step outside to settle it like a man'. It was to be a formal fight of four rounds, and they marked out boundary lines on the ground for each to keep within. Round One saw Cousens send young Tapsell sprawling to the ground; Round Two was 'a scuffling one' with no real winner. Round Three was the clincher: Tapsell struck Cousens 'a violent blow under the ear', which caused him to drop to the ground, stone dead.

On 1st September an inquest was held at the Plasterer's Arms. After a long investigation and a report of the post mortem, the coroner's jury returned a verdict of manslaughter and committed Tapsell to the next Hastings Quarter Sessions, to be held at the town hall in the High Street on 24th October.

The trial was held before the newly-appointed recorder, the Radical barrister Charles Austin ('a pale spare man of high and massive brow', who became a QC in 1841), the borough magistrates and a Grand Jury. Firstly, Ann

The foot of Castle Hill in 1818, later the site of the lime kilns.

Upton was given seven years' transportation for thieving a gold ring and some wearing apparel, then a man was sent to Lewes House of Correction for a year for stealing a piece of bacon. Finally, the most important case was heard: Tapsell was tried for 'killing and slaying' Cousens 'in a pugilistic contest'. He was sentenced to a mere two weeks in Hastings Gaol. This sentence was light because Cousens participated in the fight entirely of his own accord — in fact he was the challenger — and was expected to pay the consequences.

The unfortunate widow, Ann Cousens, was left to raise her large brood alone. She must have struggled to support them on her paltry earnings; the only employment open to women was low-paid drudgery, so Ann worked firstly as a charwoman and later as a laundress. Nevertheless she managed to raise her children well; some gained apprenticeships, others entered trades and one, her eldest, Mary Ann, emigrated alone to Australia in 1841, a brave venture indeed, especially for a girl who suffered from (as her documents stated) 'shrivelled legs'.

George Tapsell served his fortnight in jail and joined the merchant navy in 1840. Nothing more is known of his life.

References: *Bell's Life* 3 December 1826; *Sussex Advertiser* 8 January 1827; *The Globe* 25 August 1836; *Brighton Gazette* 27 October 1836; *Sussex Advertiser* 31 October 1836.

1846–1851

SACRIFICED TO THE IRON ROAD

Prior to 1846 everyone arriving in Hastings or St Leonards came by foot, on horseback or by horse-drawn vehicle. A railway line from London to Brighton opened in 1841, and from it a branch laid in early 1842 took trains to Tonbridge, from where horse-drawn coaches carried passengers to Hastings. By August a line under construction from London to Dover had reached Staplehurst. For the next four years, the easiest way to get to Hastings was to take a train fifty-three miles to Staplehurst then continue by road for the remaning twenty-three miles. This was the speediest route that had ever existed between London and our town: it took only six hours.

Local landowners and civic officers held numerous meetings to discuss the best way to bring a railway line to Hastings. A branch from Staplehurst was the most logical, but the earthworks would be costly. A line along the coast from Brighton was quicker and cheaper to build, apart from the last two miles between Bopeep and Hastings. That hilly section would require two years of expensive and difficult works, including two tunnels — one of them three-quarters of a mile long — which involved blasting with gunpowder, extensive hand-digging, and laying sixteen million bricks.

The opening of the line from Brighton to St Leonards was 'most anxiously looked forward to; and many will hail with pleasure the day when the sound of the engine may greet their ears in this hitherto isolated district', wrote one observer, whilst another said it would place Hastings 'within the reach of the invalid, as well as of the pleasure-seeker.' For the first few months the line terminated at Bulverhythe, near the recently demolished New England Bank Inn.[1] A temporary terminus, described as a 'ramshackle structure', was erected close to the sea, just east of the Bull Inn, and a horse-drawn omnibus service would provide a shuttle service to St Leonards and Hastings — our area's first bus replacement service due to engineering works!

At 11.20am on Saturday 27th June 1846 the first train arrived at Bulverhythe. Crowds of spectators assembled and coaches, flys and omnibuses waited to meet the first passengers ever to arrive in St Leonards by train. Every window on the route to Hastings was filled with spectators watching the pioneer passengers pass by. A carnival atmosphere prevailed: the town band was engaged to play all day, flags were flown, the bells of St Clements rang out with merry peals, and the town's cannon were fired to mark the historic moment. Groups of

1. T.B. Brett wrote a poem about the removal of the inn: 'Where sailors, soldiers, smugglers all/Hob nobbed in days of yore;/ That wayside inn whose site just now/ The railway covers o'er.'

Advert from the pre-railway days. How to get to Hastings in 1841.

The first railway timetable published for Hastings-bound passengers. There were four trains a day to Brighton.

revellers feasted at the major hotels, where 'Success to the Railroad' was toasted. That night a celebratory display of fireworks was held on Gingerbread Green (now The Green) and lighted tar-barrels were rolled down the hill to the beach, eliciting squeals of delight. Over the next three days, an astonishing 900 people took a train from Bulverhythe, keen to be a part of this unique event. The new line shaved a whopping two hours off the journey to London, which could now be reached in a mere four hours.

Five months later, after bridges were built over the River Asten (Combe Haven) and the road we now call the A259, the line was extended a mile to a spot levelled to accommodate a station, sidings and an engine shed.[2] It was named Bopeep, after the nearest landmark, an inn with that name.

The railway revolutionised travel to and from Hastings, and much praise, gratitude and accolades were bestowed upon the promoters, directors and chief engineers. However, the armies of navvies were largely forgotten. During the construction works their presence made a huge impact on the towns, and locals would stand and watch them working. At Bopeep,

> Upwards of 80 men were vigorously engaged in levelling the hill on which the workshops, &c, are to stand...we were astonished to see what the brawny arms of these stalwart navvies had effected.

Sometimes the wealthy residents and visitors were so impressed that they had a whip-round to give the men a treat:

> A subscription having been entered into, at St Leonards, for the purpose of giving a small reward to the labourers employed on the railroad on the occasion of its being opened, in consequence of their having generally conducted themselves in a quiet and orderly manner during the progress of the works in this neighbourhood, the proceeds were expended in bread, cheese and beer for upwards of 160 men, who were regaled in a temporary booth near the Bopeep public-house, which Mr Paine, the worthy landlord, had decorated with boughs for the occasion. The scene was also enlivened by Elford and Elliot's excellent band.

Not all navvies were unskilled labourers; many carpenters and — especially — brick-makers and bricklayers were needed, as were excavators experienced in blasting rock with explosives. The men had worked on earlier lines, and would move on to new ones when their work here was done.

They remained in the Hastings area for up to five years as they built the permanent way, with its many junctions, sidings, tunnels, embankments and bridges on three routes, the other two went to Ashford and to Tonbridge. To

2. It was later moved slightly east and renamed St Leonards West Marina. This station and depot survived until 1967. The site was opposite where Poundstretcher is today.

Looking east along the line from Bulverhythe to the portal of Bopeep Tunnel. This c1930 image illustrates that even a relatively 'easy' section of track required the digging and removal of thousands of tons of earth to make a cutting and a flat trackbed.

reach Winchelsea two tunnels had to be bored: one of 1200 yards running under the Ridge and a shorter one under Mount Pleasant Road, as well as a massive embankment across the Priory Valley. The five miles of track from Bopeep to Battle necessitated the creation of fourteen cuttings and thirteen embankments. The valleys were 'precipitous, and of a loose and boggy character' and the excavations as far as Whatlington required the removal of about 1.25million cubic yards of earth.

The total number of navvies who worked in the Hastings area was estimated at 3,500, making a dramatic impact on an area whose population was only 17,000.[3] For the first time, the town was filled with vast numbers of labouring men, and strange accents from Devon, Norfolk, Wiltshire and Ireland were heard in the streets, the beershops and the provision stores.

Such a massive influx of rough, tough, coarse-mannered men led to an exponential rise in crime (mostly the theft of food and clothing, often from other navvies) and in drunken, outdoor punch-ups. The scraps were generally with their confrères, although in 1850 there was a massive fist-fight between navvies and fishermen on the East Hill, about which a reporter remarked that, 'in showing the extent of their pugilistic powers they certainly succeeded in displaying their stupidity and ignorance by mercilessly beating one another until they were black and blue.' 'The whole scene was one of confusion and riot', he continued. P.C. Waters 'had his clothes torn to pieces, and after being kicked about for some time by a band of ruffians', a navvy 'threatened to pitch him over the cliff', although in reality here merely flung him 'over the brow of a hill into some bushes'. During the skirmish other policemen found themselves the victims of 'sundry blows, black eyes, and bruises'.

3. It was said that there were more railway navvies in England than men in the army and navy.

One observer remarked that the town was 'inundated by railway labourers, who indulged in every kind of dissipation'. T.B. Brett recorded seeing 'navvies quarrelling and fighting and others lying intoxicated on the parades and in the streets'. One day George Lindridge, a genteel church organist, was obliged to drive his carriage, containing his mother, wife and child, through a crowd of navvies brawling on the parade at St Leonards. His horse took fright and dashed off at great speed, causing the carriage to crash into a column of the Colonnade. The entire family was pitched into the road and poor Mr Lindridge was knocked unconscious for several hours.

Brett remarked that many navvies were 'really respectable and trustworthy workers', and a reporter noted that the crime rate in Hastings was low, despite 'the large number of railway labourers who are continually lounging about our streets'. This he attributed partly to the railway missionaries who gave the men Bible readings and other religious instruction. but also to the magistrates, who exhibited 'praiseworthy firmness' by inflicting 'the utmost penalty the law will allow'.

Being so numerous, inevitably the navvies struggled to find suitable lodgings. Once all the cheap rooms to let were taken, they piled into barns, sheds and haylofts, and some were discovered sleeping in net huts or snuggling up to livestock in cowsheds. Impoverished locals, led by 'the desire to make a shilling or two' would let rooms to them, and if possible, squeeze two or three into each bed. To ease the situation dozens of temporary wooden huts, or 'shanties' were erected by the contractors. The 1851 census shows a typical hut housing a navvy, his wife, two or three children and a few fellow navvies as lodgers. In 1850 seven huts in Ore caught fire and were burned to the ground; luckily nobody was hurt and so it could be enjoyed as an unusual spectacle.

Once their work was done, the navvies were usually moved on or kept in the background whilst the directors and civic dignatories held self-congratulatory opening ceremonies. However, they were sometimes permitted to play a suitably humble part in the proceedings. For example, on 28th October 1850 Mount Pleasant Tunnel and Hastings Tunnel were lined with hundreds of navvies, each holding aloft a candle, who were instructed to give 'three deafening cheers' as the Lord Mayor of London performed the ceremony of inserting the final brick, using a specially-commissioned, beautifully-inscribed silver trowel with which to pretend to press in the mortar.[4]

It comes as no surprise that T.B. Brett, that great chronicler of life in nineteenth-century Hastings, was fascinated by the coming of the railways, and, as always, he did not overlook the human element but recorded and described some of the many accidents that befell the navvies. The following compilation was gleaned from his reports, and amply illustrates how terribly dangerous the work was.

4. Thomas Farncomb, Lord Mayor of London, was invited because he was born in St Leonards. Thanks to Steve Peak, in 2020 the trowel was acquired for Hastings Museum.

Typical navvies' trucks for collecting and removing spoil whilst creating a cutting or tunnel.

Navvies using horse-drawn tipping trucks.

ACCIDENTS IN 1849

In September Mr Bonniface was greatly injured by falling from a plank in the cutting at Three Oaks Farm and Thomas Foord was partly buried by about five tons of earth falling on him. Another man was seriously hurt on the head and chest in no.3 shaft of Ore tunnel. On the same day a wagon-break gave way in Hastings tunnel, and the wagons ran forward on the horses, which caused them to kick and plunge, whereby one horse was killed and another wounded. An inrush of air blew out the lights. Shouts and moans were heard, and when lights were again procured, it was found that two lads (Stephen Styles and David Mepham) had been run over by the trucks and trampled upon by the horses, one of them suffering from a compound fracture of the right thigh and the left leg. The other lad had one leg broken. In November George Lee lost one eye, with a probability of losing the other, whilst blasting in Ore tunnel.

ACCIDENTS IN 1850

In January Francis Cook and Edward Harris were seriously hurt by a fall of earth. The latter broke his collar-bone from being thrown against a wagon-wheel. In February a labourer had a leg broken by being run over by a wagon in Bopeep tunnel. In May a man was seriously injured in the tunnel by a collision of some trucks. It caught his leg, threw him down and broke his thigh-bone.

Mr Clark fell in Ore tunnel from the centering to the floor and got a deep wound in one leg from a large nail. A boy named Friend had a muscle partly torn from one leg through being caught against the bumper-board at the tip in the Priory Meadow. Mr Macdonald was greatly injured in the head and hand by a truck in the Ore tunnel colliding with him. In July, former Polish Army Captain Ignacy Lisiecki, a political refugee, had a nasty accident whilst mounting a train of empty trucks in motion at the Priory: he fell under the wheels and received severe injuries from three trucks passing over his legs.

In September James Bryant was run over by a wagon carrying 12,000 bricks. His leg was amputated. In October James Altey sustained a broken leg caused by a fall of earth and Luke Young was injured at the Priory by a wagon falling on him. In December Richard Jones was severely hurt and nearly buried by a fall of earth and Frederick Hilton, a mere lad, sustained a broken thigh, both whilst working on the line from Bopeep to Battle.

ACCIDENTS IN 1851

In February Mr Hawkins was jammed between two wagons, and Mr Lawrence, a 'breaksman', had his left foot crushed by a wheel of an engine passing over it. He bore, with great fortitude, the amputation of his leg below the knee. Frederick Leeves had a thigh broken by a fall of earth. In September two more were injured by a fall of earth in a cutting. After being jammed between two wagons at Bopeep cutting, Charles Morris underwent the amputation of an arm. In December James Chapman fractured a thigh and James Turner was buried by a fall of earth and had to be dug out; one leg was so badly crushed it was amputated. Also in December William Martin fell over a cliff and broke his thigh. His cries were heard by the inmates of a nearby hut, who took him to the infirmary.

Clearly, a large number of navvies were maimed for life by crush injuries and loss of limbs or sight. A few spectators were also hurt, the first being Master Rock, a boy (Brett said he was eight or ten) who, in May 1846, went with his granddad to watch the navvies toiling at Bulverhythe and was run over by a wagon full of earth. His leg was amputated but he survived.

FATALITIES

The total number of navvies killed here between 1846 and 1851 is unknown. From Brett and my own research, I have listed seventeen, but they are all from the same three years. Assuming the remaining two years had similar numbers, the total must have amounted to about twenty-eight.[5]

The first death of a navvy occurred on 4th June 1846. Tom Smith, a sixteen-year-old horse driver, was run over by his cart. His leg was amputated and he died of nervous shock. A month later James Bates was killed when he fell 30ft whilst removing part of a cliff at Bopeep. On 23rd May 1847 one-legged workman William Waters lost his balance and fell off a wagon; he was run over and decapitated.

Unlike the war dead, railway navvies have no monuments or plaques to commemorate them and the sacrifices they made in the form of life and limb to build our iron roads.[6]

DEATHS ON THE RAILWAY WORKS IN 1849

March. Jeremiah Young was killed by falling earth at the Priory.

May. Henry Tyrell was injured at the Priory and was taken to the infirmary, where he died a week later.

May. John Dennis was found dead in no.3 shaft of Ore Tunnel.

June. Obed Ford, aged seventeen, was fatally run over by a wagon at Guestling.

5. Data for the second halves of 1846 and 1847 and for the whole of 1848 and 1851 are missing.
6. Fatal accidents to navvies were so common that, during the construction of Woodhead Tunnel (in the north of England) it was noted that their death rate was higher than that of the soldiers who fought at the Battle of Waterloo.

June. Carpenter James Sale, twenty-four years of age, while unloading poles at Bopeep station, fell and was so injured that he died in a few hours.

July. Henry French was killed in Bopeep tunnel by a stone being hurled at him by a blast explosion.

August. Peter Carlyon was killed when a 15ft x 9ft section of brickwork collapsed on him in Bopeep Tunnel.

August. John Ridge Bridger, twenty-nine, died of suffocation at Guestling.

October. James Bowyer, a boy of ten, was under a train of trucks greasing the wheels when the train started and ran him over. He died the next day.

DEATHS ON THE RAILWAY WORKS IN 1850

February. An inquest was held at the Warrior's Gate Inn on Richard Guyatt, aged nineteen, who had been fatally jammed between two wagons in Bopeep tunnel. The result of the enquiry was 'Accidental Death'.

May. James Collin fell whilst running a wagon of earth and had one leg cut nearly in two; the limb was amputated, but erysipelas set in on the other leg, which was also injured, and proved fatal.

May. An inquest was held at the Fortune of War, Priory Road, on William Geer, who was killed by falling down no.3 shaft of Ore tunnel at Bunger Hill, a distance of 180 feet.

June. William Hilton and Thomas Hewitt, carters on the railway works, were accompanying a load of timber down Old London road, and when near to Mr North's residence the skid-pan came off, and the shaft-horse not being able to hold the wagon back, Hewitt, who was riding on the shafts, jumped off, and was fatally crushed by the wheels.

October. An accident occurred in a tunnel to William Clark, thirty-four years of age, by the falling of the tail-board of a loaded wagon, thus letting him down, to be fatally run over by the next wagon.

References: *Brighton Gazette* 29 March, 5 July & 6 September 1849; *Brighton Guardian* 22 January, 20 June, 27 June & 2 July 1846; *Sussex Advertiser* 19 June & 7 August 1849, 28 May & 29 October 1850; *Hampshire Telegraph* 29 May 1847; T.B. Brett's manuscript histories. http://wiki.historymap.info/Brett_Manuscript_Histories

FATAL RAILWAY ACCIDENT.—On Thursday afternoon, the 4th instant, an accident, attended with loss of life, occurred at Bopeep, near Hastings, to a lad named Thomas Smith, about 16 years of age, who was working on the line at the time. An inquest was held at the Sea Side House, White Rock, on Saturday evening, the 6th inst., before J. G. Shorter, Es., coroner, and a respectable jury. From the evidence of William Collis and John Flinders, it appeared that the deceased was a driver, and while in the act of running with a horse and waggon loaded with earth to the tip, he accidentally stumbled and fell across the rail, the waggon passing over the thick part of his right thigh, and the lower part of the abdomen, crushing his person in a shocking manner. Mr Savery, surgeon, said the deceased was brought to the Infirmary about six o'clock on Thursday evening, and that it was found necessary to take off the limb, and that he died about eight o'clock on the following evening, of a shock of the nervous system.—Verdict, "Accidental Death"

A fatal accident occurred yesterday se'nnight on the railway works in the Priory Farm. Jeremiah Young, an excavator, belonging to Hatfield, in Herefordshire, was working with others at the bottom of the cutting, when three or four tons of mould fell in, and buried him up to the waist. An effort was at once made to extricate him; but before this could be accomplished, a second fall of earth buried him completely. In six or seven minutes he was dug out, and Mr David H. Gabb, a surgeon, who was in attendance, attempted to bleed him and restore consciousness, but without success. He was suffocated. Deceased has left a wife and family.

Another inquest was held at the Wheatsheaf, before J. G. Shorter, Esq., coroner for the Borough, on the body of Henry French. Deceased was one of the miners in the western shafts of the St. Leonards railway tunnel; and the miners in the shaft east of the one of which deceased worked in the drift way had occasion to blast. As it was known that the heading was nearly through, the men on the west side were warned to be careful. Deceased sat down on a barrow; and when the explosion took place, it drove the earth into the west portion of the heading, where a large stone struck him on the head and face. He was taken up as speedily as possible; but life was found to be extinct. The jury returned a verdict of "Accidental death."

GUESTLING.

An inquest was held before N. P. Kell, Esq., last week, on the body of John Ridge Bridger. James Duffy, of Ore, labourer, deposed that on the 25th August, he was at work on the railway cutting at the Rook's Farm, on the Rye and Hastings Railway, with about 40 other men. He was on the top "lift," when he observed a slide, and gave an alarm, but before deceased, who was working in the gullet below, could get away, he was overwhelmed. Deceased cried out, but a second slide of earth came down immediately and buried him. It was nearly two hours before he was extricated; and he was then quite dead. All the rest of the men got away in time to avoid injury. George Brown, ganger, in the employ of Messrs. Hoof and Sons, the contractors, attributed the slide to a perpendicular vein of sand, the existence of which was unknown to the men, giving way. Mr George Fry, surgeon, of St. Leonards, Hastings, examined the body, and attributed death to slow suffocation. The jury returned a verdict of "Accidental death."

An inquest was taken on Monday at the Warrior's Gate Inn, before J. G. Shorter, Esq., coroner for the borough, on view of the body of Peter Carlyle, a minor, aged 30, engaged in the western part of the tunnel between Bopeep and the London Road. John Leonard, who lives in London Road, stated that deceased and himself were miners on the railway works. On Saturday morning they were at work at No. 5 shaft, and as they were going home they went to see how the bricklayers were getting on in the tunnel, when, without any warning, "a length" fell in, bringing with it the whole of the supports and a part of the brickwork. He believed it was the water behind which caused the work to fall. They were standing on a scaffold when the slip came. They both jumped off, but the earth and bricks followed and buried them. Deceased being nearer the middle of the fall was completely buried; witness all but his face, which was left free.—Richard Carlyle, brother to deceased, stated that he assisted to get his brother out. He was quite dead.—William Jerman, ganger to No. 6 pit, thought the accident was occasioned by the water coming down on the brickwork; it had forced out a space 15 feet by 9 feet.—The verdict was "Accidental Death."

An inquest was held on Friday at the Pilot Inn, before J. G. Shorter, Esq., Coroner for the borough, to ascertain the cause of the death of James Bowyer. The boy was run over by a waggon on the railway works north of the Priory on the previous Wednesday; and died from the internal injuries arising from the accident. The verdict was "Accidental Death."

The Bull Inn at Bulverhythe, looking east. Sketched by C.A. Graves in 1866. The train is going from Bopeep towards Bexhill.

The 'permanent way' as it passes through Bulverhythe, showing The Bull Inn.

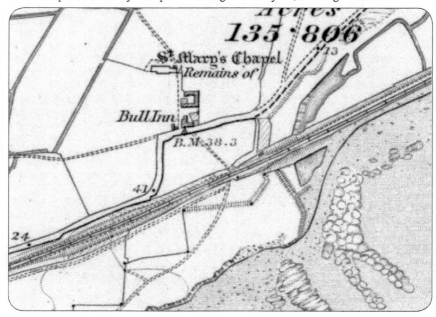

A sketch looking from the top of Castle Hill across Wellington Square in 1852. Hastings station is in the top right corner). It was completely isolated, as none of the roads that later grew up around it had yet been built. With a magnifying glass you can glimpse the portal of Hastings Tunnel. *Illustrated London News.*

Looking south-east towards Hastings station sketched from where Braybrooke Road is today. From a lithograph by Graf. The station was opened on 13th February 1851.

Caroline Hyland	Head	U	26	Dress maker
Rachel D.°	Sister	U	22	Launderess
Esther D.°	Sister	—	14	
John G Tonbridge	Lodger	U	24	Bricklayer
Alfred Cruttenden	D.°	U	18	Brick maker
Charles D.°	Head	Mar	27	D.° D.°
June D.°	Wife	Mar	22	
Sarah D.°	Daur	—	1	
Mary A Cruttenden	Daur	—	3m	
William Berrey	Head	Mar	51	Waggoner
Mary D.°	Wife	Mar	46	

11 Norman Road West (now 55 Norman Road) is an eight-roomed, three-storey house. The 1851 census, above, shows that Caroline, Rachel and Esther had two lodgers, John Tunbridge and Alfred Cruttenden and also let part of the house to two other families, a total of eleven residents.

In 1853 Rachel married John Tunbridge. They lived in the house for about thirty years, using the ground floor as a greengrocer shop. The 1881 census shows them with the first seven of their eight children, and letting other parts of the house to two couples, one with a baby.

John G Tunbridge	Head	Mar	44		Greengrocer	
Rachel Tunbridge	Wife	Mar		42	to	Wife
John G Tunbridge	Son	Unm	16		Assistant	
Edward Tunbridge	Son		14		to	
Albert A Tunbridge	Son		11		Scholar	
Harry Tunbridge	Son		9		to	
Thomas Tunbridge	Son		7		to	
Mary A Tunbridge	Daur			4	to	
Elizabeth Tunbridge	Daur			2		
James Gardiner	Head	Mar	34		Tailor	
Ann Gardiner	Wife	Mar		39		
Alfred Tollett	Head	Mar	35		Painter	
Eliza Tollett	Wife	Mar		26	to	Wife
Alfred J Tollett	Son			6m		

1849

A Pig of a Day

Norman Road

Stephen Bradley, born in Kent in 1812, apprenticed as a pork butcher. At age twenty-two rather bravely married a widow ten years his senior who had four children under the age of eight. With his new, 'ready-made' family to support he moved to Hastings, renting a house on Spittleman's Down (now called Bohemia), where they produced seven more children.

In those days it was commonplace for families to keep and fatten a pig in their garden or backyard, feeding it on scraps, then killing it for food. On 14th January 1849 Stephen was called to the Hylands' home at 11 (now 55) Norman Road West, to slaughter a hog. He hung it on a hook to let the blood drain, and returned the following evening to divide it into joints, chops, trotters, offal and sweetbreads.

Her parents being absent, Caroline Hyland, aged twenty-four, showed him through to the back yard. Night had fallen, so she held an oil lamp aloft for him to work by. He laid the hog across a large wooden table, slit it down the middle and proceeded to deploy his well-practiced skills. Plunging his knife deep into the carcase he drew it towards him with all the brute force needed to slice through the skin and muscle. When it reached a section of soft fat that overhung the table it sped through it like the proverbial hot knife through butter, and before he could take evasive action, stabbed him in the thigh.

Stephen pulled out the knife, let it clatter onto a flagstone, backed himself onto the doorstep and sat down. 'I have cut myself dreadfully', he told Caroline, and asked for a doctor. For a few seconds she wondered if he was joking, but when he saw her sister come out he exclaimed 'Oh God, I am a ruined man!' then fell silent. He had asked specifically for ex-army surgeon Robert Cumming and so Esther, aged eleven, was despatched to his home at nearby 29 Marina. Meanwhile Caroline and Rachel stood staring at Stephen, horrified by the amount of blood he was losing and yet utterly clueless about first aid.

Mr Ticehurst[1] happened to be at Cumming's house when Esther arrived, so he tagged along, as did 'chymist' George Johnson of 12 Marina. When they got to the yard Stephen had fallen forward onto his face. Turning him over carefully they searched his trouser legs for the spot where the knife had entered. They found it quickly, but there was nothing they could do: he had severed his femoral artery and was already dead.

---

1. Frederick Ticehurst (1810–1877) appears in other chapters. When this accident happened, he was deeply embroiled in the Geering triple-murder case (see Volume One).

The inquest was held the next day at the Warrior's Gate public house. Coroner J.G. Shorter and a jury (whose foreman was, rather appropriately, Samuel A. Bacon,[2] proprietor of the South Saxon Hotel) examined the scene of the tragedy. To spare his mother, Stephen's nineteen-year-old stepson identified the body.

After Caroline gave her deposition, Mr Ticehurst said that, had there been 'a man'[3] present with sufficient knowledge and presence of mind, Stephen's life could easily have been saved by the application of a thumb on the correct spot, or a tourniquet tied above the wound.

> The femoral artery is about as large as a goose quill, and is the principal blood vessel between the heart and the leg so that when it was opened every palpitation of the heart sends out a quantity of blood, so that in less than ten minutes the whole blood in the man's body was out of him — the heart was completely dried.[4]

Stephen's widow Elizabeth had lost a second husband in the prime of his life. She had eight children still living at home, of which five were too young to work. The poor woman had somehow to support them by scraping a meagre living as a laundress, one of the handful of occupations open to women who had no trade. The 1851 census sees her living at 27 Bohemia Terrace with five of her children. Just two years later she was dead. Her youngest child survived only three more years and another died three years after him. Two others emigrated to Australia and one to New Zealand.

For the Hyland girls, Stephen's shocking death was the beginning of an *annus horribilis*: by October both of their parents had died. The 1851 census shows Caroline, a dressmaker, as Head of Household at the age of twenty-six; she married in 1854 and moved out. The month Esther turned fifteen, she fell pregnant by a local carpenter's apprentice. They married when she was expecting a second child, moved to London and added eight more children to the overpopulated East End.

Rachel continued living at 11 Norman Road West for another quarter-century, seeing its number change to 55 and the 'West' dropped. She and her husband John Tunbridge raised a family of eight children there, and used the ground floor to sell fruit and veg; they were doubtless patronised by T.B. Brett, who lived almost opposite. Their son took over the house and shop and remained living and working there into the 1890s.

---

2. Yes, *Bacon*. I promise that I am not making it up.
3. Clearly he could not envisage that one day women would be doctors, battlefield nurses, etc.
4. *Sussex Advertiser* 23 January 1849.

1851

GUESTLING

THIRTEEN TIMES TWO

The two 'exits' in this chapter occurred in Guestling before and after, and within a mile of, the infamous Geering murders, which are covered in Volume One. In contrast to the substantial and extensive press coverage given to the murders, these two deaths, though equally shocking, received, between them, just one press report in one local paper.

David Foster and Harriet Beney were married at St Helen's church, Ore, on 11th July 1827, when he was twenty-eight and she eighteen, and set up home on Friar's Hill in Guestling. David became gardener to wealthy landed proprietor George Gustavus Monck, a grandson of 5th Viscount Boyne. Harriet gave birth to eight children, losing one in infancy, and then died in September 1843. For six months the elder children looked after the younger four, who were aged under ten, then in March 1844 David married Sarah Booth, a widow aged forty with no children of her own.

On 18th February 1847 one of the children hanged himself in a barn at Rock Farm, owned by James Rollason.[1] Brett provided this scanty information, and official records confirm the death of a James Foster, aged thirteen. No inquest report has yet been found, so the circumstances are shrouded in mystery.[2]

In the space of eight years the Foster children lost their mother, brother, and all four of their grandparents. When the eldest siblings moved into Hastings, they left three girls Mary (fifteen), Ann (thirteen) and Charlotte (eleven) at the mercy of their stepmother.

Homes in Guestling had no water supply (nor gas, electricity or drainage). To obtain fresh drinking water, someone had to carry a pail to a natural spring one-third of a mile away, and lug it back, full, uphill all the way, hopefully without spilling too much.

On 25th July 1851 Sarah sent Ann and Charlotte to fetch a pail of water, a chore which was 'a repetition of previous errands'. En route to the spring there was a pond by the roadside, where the girls filled the pail 'to save toiling up the hill'. For this, Ann, being the elder, was given a severe beating by her stepmother, and threatened with further punishment if she repeated the transgression. The next day the sisters were obedient, and fetched the water from the spring. On their return journey they sat down for a rest near the pond. Ann asked Charlotte

1. Who also appears in 'The Roebuck and the Bull'.
2. Sadly, the editions of the *Sussex Advertiser* from January to June 1847 are not available.

to 'mind the pail' for a few minutes, and went through some trees and out of sight. Charlotte heard a splash of water, and went to the pond, where she found her sister's bonnet lying on the ground. She ran home and their neighbours dragged the side of the pond nearest the road, but Ann was not found.

The next morning P.C. George Jeffery dragged the far side of the pond, which was overhung by trees, and there discovered the girl's lifeless body.

The inquest was held at the nearby White Hart Inn by Coroner Kell.[3] Neighbour Matilda Cloke deposed that Sarah worked the children so hard that locals dubbed them 'The Little Slaves'. Her daughters Harriet, twelve, and Mary, eight, along with Alice Willard, fourteen, detailed the ill-treatment Sarah meted out to the girls: she made them carry heavy loads of wood and water and hit them for the smallest transgression. Mary Foster, fifteen, revealed that three weeks earlier Sarah had given Ann a severe beating. However, David and Sarah denied it. Ann's eldest sister, Harriet, twenty-one, a domestic servant to a grocer on Old London Road, said she had discussed Sarah's ill-treatment of her sisters with her Aunt Sophia, who told her that she heard Sarah tell the girls that, if they were tired of fetching water, they 'might go and drown themselves' to get out of the chore. When Sophia gave her deposition, she denied saying it.

The jurymen concluded that Ann had committed suicide 'while in an unsound state of mind'. Significantly, they added: 'We beg to express our decided opinion that extreme severity has been used by the father and stepmother towards the deceased and her sister, and which we most severely censure'. These were strong words, and revealing ones, too, because at the time it was perfectly legal, acceptable and indeed routine to use physical punishment to 'correct' children. The Fosters must have been brutal to incite such a comment.

After the tragic suicides of two children within four years, both at a shockingly young age, life went on for the Fosters. The 1861 census shows the couple living with Mary and Charlotte. However, by 1871 all four led separate lives. Charlotte married a bricklayer and Mary became a domestic servant and had an illegitimate child by her employer. David became gardener to wealthy widow Mary Ann Thatcher, the mother-in-law of surgeon Frederick Ticehurst, and lived on site at The Plantation, Fairlight, whilst Sarah lived alone elsewhere. She died, aged seventy-six, in 1881. That year's census lists David in Hastings Union Workhouse in Cackle Street, where he died two years later.

References: T.B. Brett_Volume 4, Chapter XLVI. *Sussex Advertiser* 29 July 1851.

3. Nathaniel Polhill Kell (1792-1864), coroner for the Rape of Hastings from 1838 until his death. As an attorney-at-law he took into partnership a young Charles Sheppard, who 'inherited' the coronership from him. Both men appear in both volumes of *Strange Exits*.

Death Leap

Railway line, Bexhill

Elizabeth Carey was born in east London in 1785. At some point she moved to Rye, where in 1807 she married musician William Coleman Edwards. The couple had nine children, then William died. Elizabeth urgently needed to find a way to support her family, three of whom were under six years old, so she moved to St Leonards and founded a 'dame' school (a small infants' school inside a private home). Initially based in Shepherd Street, by 1851 she moved to 45 Norman Road West and was listed in the census as a schoolmistress with two grown up daughters, both dressmakers. The family lived near the Hylands and must have known them.[1]

On Friday 26th March 1852 Elizabeth, then sixty-six, set out to visit her daughter Maria, a domestic servant to the upper crust Lane family at Broadoak Manor[2] one-and-a-half miles walk from Bexhill station. She intended to ask her to resign and become housekeeper to her brother Edward, who was newly widowed and needed someone to keep house and look after his children.He was a pastry cook with a shop in Norman Road, and doubtless his comestibles were savoured by T.B. Brett, who lived at no.17.

The nearest station was Gensing (now Warrior Square) but trains from Hastings to Bexhill did not stop there (they would after 1870) so Elizabeth went to St Leonards station, situated where Carpetright is today.[3]

There were five trains a day, and Elizabeth travelled by the fourth, which left Hastings at 4.45pm. The last train back departed at 7.43pm, giving her two hours to persuade her daughter to come home. She bought a third class ticket from the station master, thirty-year-old Joshua Bennett, who noted that she was 'perfectly calm and rational', and was politely ushered into the rear carriage by Porter William Grey. It was an open carriage with sides and doors, but no roof, and wooden benches for seats. She was the only occupant.

When the train arrived at Bexhill the guard called out the station name (they did this for the benefit of those who could not read name-boards). Station master John Heild approached Elizabeth because she was standing up, 'leaning her arms over the off side of the carriage, looking at the station house'. He asked if she wished to alight. She gave no reply, but sat down and looked away. The

1. See 'Pig of a Day'.
2. Broadoak is long since demolished; Deerswood Lane covers the site. Colonel Henry Lane, a county magistrate, appears in 'The Wicked Stepmother'.
3. It was moved east in 1880, renamed St Leonards West Marina, and closed in 1967.

train sat in the station for a minute, giving her ample time to get off, then the guard gave the engine driver the flag signal to go, and Mr Heild watched the train depart. When it was about fifty yards distant he saw Elizabeth rise from her seat, pace the carriage and wave her hand in the air. She seemed agitated and he wondered if she had dropped something over the side. Then the train followed a curve in the track and disappeared from his view.

Platelayer Dennis found Elizabeth a mile west of Bexhill station, lying face down on the down line, 200 yards from Reeve's cattle arch. She was alive, but bleeding from the nose and mouth. He called to a passer-by for help in moving her to a safe place, then fetched Mr Heild and Frederick Wallis, a nearby surgeon, who wanted her carried to The Bell in Church Street. They lifted her onto a litter, where she expired, securing her place in history as the first local to be killed by falling out of a passenger train.

The accident aroused enormous public interest. A well-regarded older resident had lost her life using a new-fangled mode of transport that many felt instinctively was unsafe. People who had hitherto gone everywhere by foot or, if they were lucky, in a horse-drawn vehicle going at a leisurely pace, or a lightweight fly trotting through town, were understandably wary of the huge, noisy, scary 'iron horses' which hauled flimsy-looking wooden carriages at what appeared to be breakneck speed and whose braking systems were questionable. Her death had serious implications for everyone who needed to know whether it was safe for themselves and their loved-ones to travel on the railway.

At 1pm on Tuesday 30th March Coroner Kell opened the inquest at The Bell, a long-established coaching inn, by excusing his late attendance. It was customary for an inquest to be held the day after a death, but in this case four days had passed. Kell explained that he had been staying in Essex, and a letter posted from his office in Battle on Friday had taken two days to reach him. He scheduled the inquest for 11am on Tuesday, but got the train times muddled, which was why he was two hours late.

The foreman of the jury reproached Mr Kell: the sons of the deceased had been waiting for him at The Bell since Saturday. One had even ridden to Kell's office to find out what was going on. The foreman suggested, sarcastically, that Kell 'appoint a deputy' to cover for him. Kell flinched at the man's rebuke and replied tartly that Lord Chichester appointed him 'with the express condition' that he conduct all inquests himself, and for this one he had undergone the inconvenience of a 200-mile round trip.

Elizabeth's sons had engaged a solicitor and the London, Brighton & South Coast Railway sent theirs to quash any attempt to blame the company. The *Sussex Advertiser* report filled two full columns of broadsheet, which indicated how significant the case was to the public. Newspapers as far away as Exeter, Newcastle and Liverpool also reported the inquest.

The doctor's opinion that Elizabeth died of 'compression of the brain, caused by concussion' was straightforward, but the court then spent four hours trying to work out how and why she ended up on the track. The coroner interrogated every railwayman, no matter how small his interaction with her and it was clear that she had been given ample chance to alight. She was alone in the carriage so there were no witnesses, nor indeed anyone who could have attacked her, or flung her out. She must have leapt out of her own accord. Because rail travel was new, people were as yet unable to judge the perils of jumping out of a moving vehicle. The jury concluded that it was an accident.

On 2nd April Elizabeth was buried alongside her husband at Rye.

Newspapermen extolled her many virtues. One reported that she was 'much respected in the vicinity for her quiet, neighbourly habits.' She had raised her children to be decent, hardworking people, and each was a great credit to her. William trained as an accountant and acted as a casual newspaper reporter whilst Edward became a master confectioner with a busy shop on Rye High Street, stocked by his own bakery. He also served as an overseer, a special constable, and as Grand Master of the Oddfellows. After moving to Hastings he built an equally thriving business in St Andrew's Road (now Queen's Road), which he ran with his second wife Eliza and their daughter, Jane, until his death.

The 1851 census for 45 Norman Road West. The household comprised Mrs Edwards and her daughters Elizabeth, a milliner, and Harriette, a dressmaker. With them is Edward's daughter Jane, whose mother had recently died.

References: *Sussex Advertiser* 6 April 1852; *Brighton Gazette* 1 April 1852.

Alex Leadbeater's studio, 'The Muse', is thought to be the only remaining example of the stables with rooms above in Harold Mews.

A map showing Harold Mews in the 1870s.

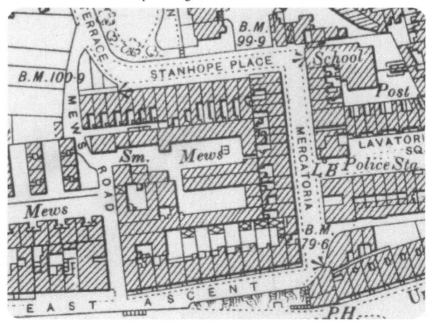

1853

MURDER IN THE MEWS

HAROLD MEWS

In the 1850s many wealthy and privileged people moved to the new and fashionable town of St Leonards, and yet, hidden behind some of the spacious and beautifully appointed houses, many impoverished locals lived in squalor. Among them were Stephen Smith, known as 'Bogy', born in Bexhill about 1811, and his girlfriend Sarah, a year or so his senior. Her father was a well known fisherman called 'Toot' Taught, and, according to the *Sussex Advertiser*, her family 'have dwelt in Hastings since the days of Queen Elizabeth'.

Although Sarah claimed to have wed 'at the old church in Brighton' in 1835, the parish register bears no trace of this, and local gossips whispered that Sarah merely 'passed' as his wife. The first time the couple was recorded together was in the 1851 census, which listed them in Market Street, a gloomy back-street behind Grand Parade. They occupied no.7, next door to the Saxon Shades, which was on the eastern corner. When they moved out in April 1852, the neighbours were glad to see the back of them:

> Her unfortunate husband and herself have been known to quarrel violently, so much so that for a long time they were a terror to the inhabitants.

Thomas Skinner was a riding master (someone who taught horse riding) and the proprietor of horse-drawn vehicles for hire, including flys, wagonettes and pony phaetons. When he moved his business to Harold Mews it became known as Skinner's Mews, and in the early days he and his family also resided there, in the best house on the corner. It consisted of an E-shaped yard containing a number of coach houses and stables. Each had a room above, to provide overnight accommodation for visiting coachmen; however, Skinner let six of them as cheap dwellings for locals who could afford nothing better. It was here that Stephen and Sarah lived from April 1852 until May 1853.

The couple had only one room, which measured 12ft by 6ft, and this small space had to do duty as kitchen, living room, bathroom, bedroom, and workshop. On the rough timber floorboards sat a chest of drawers, a table, a wooden chair, a work chair and, in one corner, 'a wretched bed on the floor'. They owned a few shabby clothes, some chipped crockery and a well-worn set of shoemaker's tools. The couple lived from week to week on the pittance Bogy earned from repairing shoes and boots. Only two things made their miserable existence bearable: alcohol, and the chance to escape from their comfortless hovel by spending time in the warm, convivial surroundings of the town's plentiful public houses.

On the evening of Whit Tuesday, 17th May 1853, Bogy worked until nearly 8pm then he and Sarah strolled to the Queen Adelaide beerhouse in West Street. Constable Fryman, who knew them, saw them there at about 11pm; they appeared to be happy together, and were drinking 'part of a pot of porter', but 'nothing to hurt'. On the way home Sarah gave Bogy the slip and at a quarter past midnight entered the Warrior's Gate pub and asked for a pint of beer to take away. The landlord put the beer in a can, which she promised to return the next morning.

When Sarah got home Bogy was waiting to confront her. He berated her for going off without him and demanded to know where she had been. This angered her so much that she seized an old but fearsomely sharp shoe-mender's knife and threatened to stab him with it if he did not stop going on. He responded by unbuttoning his waistcoat and shirt and pulling them apart to expose his bare chest, and then daring her to 'Do it, then!' Sarah plunged it between his ribs so forcefully that the blade slid into him right up to its hilt.

As blood poured from the wound and Bogy groaned in pain, Sarah pulled up his work chair and helped him back himself onto it. She withdrew the knife from his body and tossed it out of the window, then, walking across to their neighbour's room, rapped on the door and called out, 'Would you have the kindness to get up, Mrs Cope, for I have stabbed my Steve.' The old lady climbed out of bed and went to the Smiths' room. Bogy was seated on his old wooden chair, clutching a blood-soaked shoemaker's apron to his chest. Sarah was pacing up and down in an agitated fashion, saying, 'I have murdered him, and I meant to do it', to which Mary Cope exclaimed, 'Oh, you wicked woman!'

Still in her nightgown Mrs Cope returned to her room, threw on a shawl and hurried out of the mews, down Mews Road and East Ascent to Marina, where she rang the doorbell of no.51, the home of a young surgeon, Roger Cooper Gardiner.[1] As it was 1.30am he was fast asleep, but his servant answered the door and woke him with the urgent message. Mr Gardiner dressed quickly and accompanied Mrs Cope back to the mews.

By then Sarah had placed a pillow under Bogy's head and had made an attempt to close and cleanse the wound. Seeing Mr Gardiner she confessed: 'I have killed my husband, I knew it would come to this.' But Bogy was not dead; as the doctor was assessing his injury he breathed two or three times, then fell silent. Sarah repeatedly asked, 'Is he dead?' Mr Gardiner nodded and asked her for the weapon, but she could not produce it. She was terribly agitated and Mr Gardiner feared she was 'meditating self-destruction', especially as she glanced

1. Gardiner also appears in 'The Case of Hannah Moore' on page 184.

ST. LEONARDS-ON-SEA.

DISTRESSING CASE OF MURDER.—A MAN KILLED BY HIS WIFE.

Very great excitement prevailed in this town on Wednesday morning, consequent upon a report that a man named Stephen Smith *alias* "Bogy," by trade a shoemaker, had been stabbed during the night by his wife. The report spread rapidly, and very little enquiry proved that it was unfortunately true.

At the rear of the row of houses known as the East Ascent, is some stabling, the most northern, part of which is called the Harold Mews, and are in the occupation of Mr. T. Skinner, riding-master. Over the coach houses are a series of apartments, and in one of these resided the unfortunate man and his wife, who has become his murderess. The details of the unfortunate occurrence, will be gathered from the proceedings taken before the Bench of Magistrates, and the Coroner.

The prisoner *Sarah Smith*, aged 42, a thin woman of dissolute appearance, was brought up at the Clerk's Office at ten o'clock on Wednesday morning.

Sussex Advertiser 24 May 1853.

repeatedly towards a pile of other sharp tools on the workbench, 'as if to find another knife to do herself some harm'. Leaving Mrs Cope to guard her, he told Sarah he was going home to fetch a bandage, but instead went out to look for the local bobby on his beat.

George Burgess was patrolling near the Warrior's Gate Inn when Mr Gardiner approached and told him, 'I have got a case of murder'. They walked to Harold Mews. Seeing P.C. Burgess Sarah leapt from her chair and cried, 'Oh, dear me! Why did I do it! I have done it, and no one else, and I must be hung for it. I am a murderer; the first of the family that was ever handled by a policeman.' Burgess placed her under arrest and took her away. Mr Gardiner and Mrs Cope searched for the knife; they eventually found it on a dung-heap beneath the window, coated in wet blood. It was a shoemaker's paring knife, much worn, its wooden handle split and bound round with numerous 'wax-ends'.

As P.C. Burgess and Sarah were going through George Street towards the police station in the High Street they ran into P.C. Fryman. Sarah exclaimed, 'Oh, Fryman, I have killed my husband, but I did not mean to do it'. He accompanied them to the station house, and when Burgess went to fetch a female searcher they had a one-to-one chat; Sarah confided: 'I have taken up a knife at him manys and manys a time, but this time I meant it.' Fryman asked what she thought would become of her and she replied that she would 'be hung for it'.

After being searched, Sarah settled in to spend a few hours in the cold, grim cell, which, actually, was hardly worse than her own austere home. At 10am she was taken to the Town Clerk's Office inside the town hall in the High Street and placed in front of two magistrates, Mayor Thomas Hickes and surgeon Frederick Ticehurst, who remanded her, pending enquiries.

The inquest was held the same day at 2.30pm, in the parlour of the Horse and Groom in Mercatoria. It was conducted by a twenty-four-year-old solicitor. Robert Growse was new to Hastings, and acted as clerk to Coroner J.G. Shorter. On that day he was deputising for the deputy coroner, John Phillips.[2] He and the jury made their way through the pub's rear exit into Harold Mews, where they viewed the body. Bogy was still seated, with his head tilted back onto a pillow balanced on the top of the other chair. His chest lay bare and there was a small red slit visible. The men returned to the pub, where they heard Mr Gardiner describe the wound. It was between the fourth and fifth ribs, on the right side; the incision was jagged and the edges were bruised, as if the instrument which inflicted the wound had been driven 'right home' to the hilt, which took considerable force. The knife had pierced the pericardium and the aorta, causing haemorrhage; death followed in about fifteen minutes.

The jurymen had a brief discussion before the foreman announced their decision. 'We are quite agreed to a unanimous verdict of Wilful Murder against Sarah Smith, and, I am sorry to say, there does not appear any mitigating circumstances'.

Sarah was kept in custody overnight, and at 11am the next morning, Thursday 19th May, she was taken back to the courtroom.

> The vicinity of the Town Hall was thronged by a large concourse of persons, attracted to the vicinity from a morbid curiosity to behold a fellow-mortal, whose hands were dyed in her husband's blood; and to hear a succinct narrative of the particulars attending the commission of so heinous an offence.

Sarah arrived for her final examination and committal by magistrates Charles Clift (the Mayor), surgeons Frederick Ticehurst and Robert Ranking,[3] former mayor and past and future MP Frederick North (father of Marianne, who would one day become a famous painter), and John Manington, a wealthy, single, septuagenarian businessman of 95 High Street. She was placed in the

2. As well as being coroner and deputy, Shorter and Phillips were in partnership as solicitors at 85 High Street. Growse was Shorter's office clerk, yet was permitted to hold two murder inquests (Stephen Smith and James Wellerd). When Shorter committed suicide, Growse conducted that inquest, too. He then took over Shorter's posts as coroner and Town Clerk, and was also made Clerk of the Peace, all by the age of thirty. He married Shorter's daughter. At the age of thirty-nine he died suddenly from a chill after riding a horse on a cold day. His widow and two small sons left Hastings for London shortly afterwards.
3. Ranking also appears in 'The Fishing Boat Mystery' and 'Mud Jack's Wife'.

dock, where her personal appearance was inspected and judged local pressmen. One called her 'not at all prepossessing', and 'thin, haggard and stolid'. 'Not a trace of an emotion could be discerned on her countenance', he wrote. Another described her as 'dissolute' and 'of most forbidding appearance'. *The Times* told its readers that she was 'a loose character, of drinking habits and possessing an ungovernable temper', whilst the *Sussex Advertiser* warned that she was 'very violent at times'. Flavius Josephus Palmer, who lodged with the Smiths (in their one room!) for a month over Christmas 1852, recalled that they were 'often drunk and quarrelling'.[4] The neighbour, Mrs Cope, claimed that Sarah had a 'hot, nasty temper, particularly after having a little beer, which she was in the habit of taking.'

After Mr Gardiner, retired tailoress Mrs Cope and the two police officers gave their evidence Sarah was given the opportunity to speak. She was allowed to sit in the dock on a chair raised up on a platform, an arrangement that had been constructed for Mary Ann Geering.'[5] Contradicting her previous statement, she said she merely threw the knife at Steve, and that he admitted it was his own fault. He extracted the knife himself and asked her to chuck it out of the window. When she claimed that he had 'put his lips up to kiss me', a 'ripple of sensation went around the court'. The clerk took down her statement and she just about managed to sign it, though 'her hand shook exceedingly'. It was now time to leave, which meant facing the public.

> A great number of persons waited in High Street, to witness the prisoner's removal from the Hall to the gaol. She was taken from the Hall in a fly, and removed to Lewes by the 4.45 train, to await her trial.

Before news of the murder was reported in the press there had been an arrest, a charge, a remand hearing, a post mortem, an inquest, a magistrates' court hearing, a committal, a funeral in the burial ground of St Leonards church, and the culprit had been locked up in Lewes House of Correction.

The story first appeared on Thursday 19th May, in both *The Times* and the *Brighton Gazette*. The latter told its readers that Hastings had been 'thrown into the utmost consternation' by the incident, and pointed out the murder scene's proximity to Caterina Villa, where another murder had occurred just five years previously.[6] The story was the subject of a lengthy and detailed article in the *Sussex Advertiser* on Tuesday 24th. Provincial papers picked up the news from *The Times* and soon folk in Cornwall, Scotland, Wales and Ireland were reading about Sarah, Stephen and their shabby room above a stable in the genteel seaside town of St Leonards.

4. Flavius's family lived at 16 Lavatoria, a small terraced house (now 92 Norman Road) which in 1851 housed three families, totalling seventeen people.
5. This case is described in full in Volume One.
6. This case is also described in full in Volume One.

On 16th July Sarah was conveyed by prison van from Lewes Gaol to the court in the High Street, where the Summer Assizes were held. The judge was the Lord Chief Baron Pollock; Mr Horne and Mr Attree prosecuted for the Crown and Mr Hurst was the defence counsel.[7] The charge was that Sarah had 'feloniously, wilfully and of malice aforethought, killed and murdered Stephen Smith, her husband, by stabbing him in the breast.'

The witnesses repeated the statements they had given at the inquest and the magistrates' court. The judge explained the difference between 'premeditated malice' and manslaughter. Mr Hurst appealed to the jury to reduce the charge to manslaughter because of the 'circumstances of excitement and liquor' prevailing at the time of the 'melancholy occurrence', he asserted that the fatal blow had been inflicted 'in the heat of passion'. The jury obliged.

The judge remarked that 'a long course of drunken and quarrelsome habits' had 'destroyed the comforts of their domestic life', and the prisoner 'had been in the habit of indulging in temper, and that this crime was the consequence of that temper not having been sufficiently controlled.' He sentenced Sarah to be transported for ten years.

Sarah was sent to Lewes Gaol and House of Correction to await a government order detailing the arrangements for placing her on a ship to Australia. That day never came because, two weeks before she was sentenced, the Penal Servitude Act had been passed, which phased out transportation in favour of penal servitude. Sarah was therefore detained at Lewes.

In April 1854 Lewes Gaol was sold to the government to house prisoners of war from the Crimea.[8] It was to be handed over on 21st June, and the inmates would be moved out. Sarah would be housed in Woking Female Penitentiary. However, in May she was taken ill and placed in the infirmary. On Monday 6th June she became 'out of her mind' and babbled in an incoherent manner to Mary Banks, a fellow prisoner tasked with nursing her. About 1.30pm she fell asleep and, having 'breathed her last without a struggle', died. She was just forty-four. The coroner's jury returned a verdict of natural death caused by 'an effusion into the head'.

References: *Brighton Gazette* 19 May 1853; *The Times* 19 May 1853; *Sussex Advertiser* 24 May 1853; *South Eastern Gazette* 26 July 1853. Thanks to Alex Leadbetter for allowing me to use her photo of The Muse.

7. Pollock, Horne and Hurst were also involved in the trial of Mrs Geering in 1849 (see Vol. One).
8. It later became a naval prison.

Harold Mews

Over the years Harold Mews has accommodated stables, fly proprietors, coach-painters, blacksmiths, carpenters and motor repair workshops. It has also been the scene of poverty, lawlessness, inebriety, violence and tragedy. In 1865 a tenant drank himself to death. Ten years later a resident fly driver was convicted of drink-driving and assaulting the police. In 1885 a twelve-year-old living there was given twelve lashes of the rod for stealing bread and cucumbers. During the 1890s it was home to a fowl thief, a wife beater and a man who inflicted cruelty on a pony. A new low spot was reached when a forty year-old resident raped his neighbour's nine-year-old girl.

In 1896 a 'wandering lunatic' smashed every window in the mews before being locked up. In 1907, when the mews was in the hands of fly proprietor Edward Pope, one of his drivers was thrown off a coach and killed. Three years later Pope hanged himself inside one of the stables. By 1936 the accommodation was a century old and dilapidated. Squalor prevailed, and Cllr Tingle called it 'one of the worst places' he had ever seen. He suggested that the slum clearance programme should have started there instead of in the Old Town.

The stables have long since been demolished, save for one, which is now known as The Muse, an artist's studio. The rest is filled with a collection of mismatched sheds and lock-ups, a workshop for a lawnmower repair shop and a furniture restorer.

A row of lock-up sheds in Harold Mews in 2020, which may date back to the 1840s.

Skinners

Thomas Skinner delighted residents during the snowy winter of 1866–67 by hiring a sleigh and offering pleasure rides to townsfolk and visitors. His sons John and William continued and expanded the business he founded: they were job and posting masters, livery stable keepers and corn merchants. They left Harold Mews and set up at Sussex Mews, Eversfield Mews and Western Road. John was so proud of being hired by the Prince and Princess of Wales in 1882 that for years afterwards he boasted about it in all his adverts. Skinners remained in Western Road even as horse-drawn vehicles were phased out and motor transport took over. They provided an early public bus service, then ran a fleet of coaches for many years. The firm's name continued in Hastings into the twentieth century, and is still prominent as a large, used car dealership in Rye.

T. Skinner,
RIDING MASTER, Harold Mews, St. Leonards.
—Livery, Private, and Bait Stables.
Post Horses, Gigs, Flys, Pony Phætons, &c.

Public houses

The Saxon Shades was a beershop belonging to the Saxon Hotel. It later became the Yorkshire Grey, then the Admiral Benbow, and is now a private house.

The Horse and Groom in Mercatoria is the oldest pub in St Leonards, dating from 1829. Its name reveals its connection to the stables at the rear.

The Queen Adelaide opened in West Street soon after the widowed queen herself visited Hastings in 1837. It was a beershop which later became a public house and traded for 170 years. It closed in 2009.

The Warrior's Gate Inn was on the corner of Norman Road (the post office now occupies the site). Prior to its construction, Warrior's Gate was the name given to the area roughly between Norman Road and the east corner of Warrior Square. The name may be a corruption of 'Warehouse Gate', a warehouse being a place to hide smuggled goods. When the inn opened in 1833 it was one of the earliest in St Leonards and also offered accommodation. When London Road was built it was numbered 18. Bombed during WW2, it was rebuilt in 1950 on the corner of Shepherd Street, and has lately reopened as a pub called the St Leonard.

The former Saxon Shades, on the corner of Market Street.

1854

THE ROEBUCK AND THE BULL

HIGH STREET

The *dramatis personae* in this true tale are James Rollason, forty-nine, a farmer of sixty-eight acres of land;[1] his servants William Morris, twenty-three and James Geering, thirteen, grandson of the infamous murderer Mary Ann Geering; Henry Hards, thirty-five, landlord of the Roebuck Inn, 27 High Street; Mr Nathaniel Polhill Kell, a Battle solicitor who was coroner for the Rape of Hastings for twenty-seven years, and Mr Ticehurst, an eminent gentleman who served Hastings for half a century as a surgeon, magistrate, alderman, mayor and coroner.

On Saturday 21st October an inquest was held at Mr Rollason's house, Rock Farm, Guestling. Rollason kicked off proceedings by relating the events of Thursday morning. After breakfasting with the Rollason family, Will and James were instructed to drive the horse and cart to Hastings to collect a large quantity of dung from the Roebuck Inn stables and take it to White Hart meadows to be spread on the fields. Will was a very sober young man, he said; in three years he had never once seen him the worse for liquor. James was a very good, well-behaved boy.

James spoke next. He explained what happened at the Roebuck. They were in the yard, loading the cart with horse dung from a pit. The dung was 'very hot and smoky' and the labour very arduous. After half-an-hour the landlord kindly brought them a pint pot of porter, which the pair quaffed thirstily, Will taking the lion's share. When they finished loading and were about to leave, Will boldly asked Mr Hards if there was 'any chance' of another drink. Mr Hards was most amiable, and sent him to the bar to fetch a pint pot, which he filled from a cask in the cellar. It was jolly tasty stuff, and Will and James drank a quarter-pint each. James began to feel 'rather queer', so went to the bar for a biscuit. On his return they finished off the pot and Will rather cheekily remarked to Mr Hards, 'We must have another one, sir.' The generous landlord again obliged and, because James declined to drink any more, Will downed nearly the whole pot himself.

Suitably refreshed and having had 'one for the road' Will twitched the reins and the horse drew the cart out of the yard and into the High Street. James managed to climb up onto the cart, where he passed out cold. When he woke up he found himself at home in his bed, without a clue how he got there. Night had fallen and he felt utterly ghastly, so he went back to sleep. In the morning he discovered what had happened to his workmate.

1. Mr Rollason also appears in the chapter 'Thirteen Times Two'.

The Roebuck's frontage on High Street and (below) its back
yard photographed in 1875. The pub closed in 1918. The house
seen through the archway below is 90b High Street.

Surgeon Frederick Ticehurst told the coroner's court that he was called to Rock Farm, where he found Will and James lying on the ground near the cart. Will was covered in his own vomit, and stone dead. James was paralytic, but Mr Ticehurst was able to save him from the same fate by making him sick. Will, he said, had died of apoplexy, brought on by whatever noxious concoction the landlord had given him. For purposes of analysis Police Inspector Campbell had given Mr Ticehurst a sample taken from the same cask. The doctor described it as 'dark, nasty stuff', which, nevertheless, 'tasted very pleasant'.

Mr Hards explained that the drink he had given to the pair was something called 'bull'. This alcoholic home brew was of his own devising. It was concocted by swilling boiling water in empty gin hogsheads, rum barrels and brandy casks and then mixing the resulting grog together. It was originally created to give to hardy fishermen when they returned from a gruelling voyage. Clearly Hards had not tried the stuff himself, for he told the inquest that he was 'not at all aware of its strength'.

The coroner advised the jurymen that they had to decide whether there was 'any criminality on the part of Mr Hards'. If so, the case was one of manslaughter. They retired for a short time and, on returning, the foreman announced a verdict of 'accidental death brought on by apoplexy, through the drink given by Henry Hards'. The coroner cautioned the landlord against giving out any more 'bull' without first testing its strength.

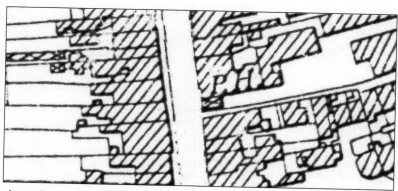

The Roebuck, marked as 'P.H.', was on the corner of an alley (or twitten) which was widened and became today's Roebuck Street. The site of the inn was lately used for a doctor's surgery and pharmacy, which are now closed.

Reference: *Sussex Advertiser* 24 October 1854.

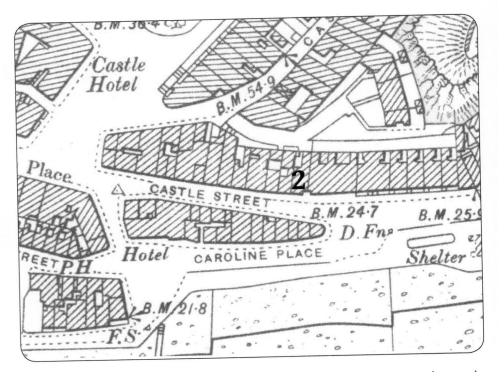

2 Castle Street comprised a commodious shop with a 16ft wide frontage, a maisonette above, and a brick-built building to the rear (presumably a cold place to store fish and hang game). The narrow sandwich shop currently next door to Iceland is no.3, but no.2 no longer exists, having long been demolished and replaced by the delightful edifice called Cavendish House.

George Stace and William Ball took over Ball's brother-in-law Richard Baldock's business in 1847, and then dissolved their partnership in 1856, giving Stace sole ownership.

Dissolution of Partnership.

WE, the undersigned WILLIAM BALL and GEORGE STACE, Fishmongers and Poulterers, and now carrying on that trade, at No. 2, Castle Street, at Hastings, in the County of Sussex, have, this 21st day of February, 1856, agreed to dissolve the said Partnership by mutual consent, on and from the 25th day of March now next ensuing.

All debts due to or owing by us to be paid or received, and the accounts adjusted at the office of Messrs. BOYKETT BREEDS & SON, No. 68, George-street, in Hastings, aforesaid.

(Signed)   WILLIAM BALL,
             GEORGE STACE,

Hastings, Feb. 21st, 1856.

FISHMONGER'S FOLLY

CASTLE HILL

George Stace's roots were wholly local. His ancestors hailed from Brede, Dallington, Crowhurst and Rye, and bore typical local surnames, including Sinden, Stonestreet, Isted and Catt. His grandfather was a country blacksmith and his father William followed the same trade in the Old Town, surrounded by the fishermen of Hastings. Perhaps growing up amongst them inspired George to break with family tradition and become a fishmonger.

George's wife came from Staffordshire. Ann Parker, a rural labourer's daughter, married her first husband at just seventeen. After being widowed or running away, she ended up in Kent and somehow met George, whom she married at St Clements in 1848.

George was in partnership with William Ball. In 1847 they had taken over an existing fish, poultry, oyster and game shop at 2 Castle Street,[1] a prominent position which they used to advantage. T.B. Brett noted that in 1854 their window 'exhibited a conger eel 6ft 4in in length and 70lb in weight'. The shop's location was perfect, because the town centre was gradually shifting westwards from the Old Town to where it is today.[2] Soon it was flanked by other popular shops and by the 1860s the street was one of the best in town.

Mr Ball left Hastings for London in 1856, leaving the business to George. He vacated the maisonette above the shop, so the Staces moved in. By March 1863 they had four sons and two daughters, the eldest aged fourteen and the youngest two, and Ann was eight months pregnant.

On Tuesday 10th March every town in the UK celebrated the wedding of the Prince of Wales to Princess Alexandra of Denmark. The morning was ushered in by the merry peals of church bells and the firing of cannon. Flags and banners were hoisted all along the seafront, shops and houses were festooned with flowers and wreaths, and banners were hung from window ledges displaying 'mottos expressive of good wishes'. A truly phenomenal triumphal arch was erected across Castle Street, formed of evergreens, garlands and flags and topped by a huge Prince of Wales feather. The streets were in 'the utmost bustle and excitement' and a gift of 1s 6d (about £7 today) was doled out to every impoverished widow and aging pauper.

1. 'Game' included pheasant, duck, ptarmigan, goose, grouse, rabbit and hare.
2. This was prompted partly by the opening of the station in 1851, and the subsequent building of shops, houses and business premises around the station area.

At 10am the town's 3,000 schoolchildren lined all four sides of Wellington Square and sang the National Anthem, accompanied by a stupendous brass band. After 'several hearty cheers' were raised, a magnificent procession, half a mile long, set out through town, complete with marching bands and banners held high, whilst spectators filled every window and balcony along the route. As each group of children arrived at their schoolroom, they found that a gala lunch had been laid out for them, the like of which they had never before seen or tasted. At noon royal salutes were fired from the various coastguard batteries, as well as from the castle. This was followed by a thrilling procession of the Cinque Ports Artillery Volunteers and Rifles. Starting from their drill hall in Middle Street they paraded proudly along the seafront to St Leonards and back, accompanied by loud brass bands playing uplifting marches all along the route. This fabulous spectacle culminated in a twenty-one gun salute.

On the West Hill, throughout the afternoon thousands of people took part in traditional English sports and games, including 'a grand donkey race, jumping in sacks, a jingling match, bobbing at treacle rolls, wheelbarrow races and climbing a greasy pole'. Hundreds of pots of beer were served in public houses whilst temperance halls offered fresh lemonade. A huge, open-air tea party was thrown by the 'jovial dames of All Saints' Street, who swung their kettles à la gipsy'. Old Towners danced gaily to the strains of a hired fiddler playing popular tunes, including that well loved classic 'The Wedding Day'.

As night fell the town hall, the Queen's Hotel and the Marine Hotel were brilliantly illuminated and no less than four hundred gas jets lit up Hastings Castle, creating a magical scene. A breathtaking torch-light procession by the fire brigade was followed by the firing of signal-guns, then, 'as though by magic, blue lights were displayed by the coastguards all along the parades'. A flight of rockets was set off from a revenue cutter floating a little way from the shore, heralding a spectacular display of pyrotechnics which lit up Eversfield Parade. 'The scene was one of enchantment', wrote eyewitness T.B. Brett.

The climax of this day of 'unbounded enjoyment' was a grand bonfire on the summit of Castle Hill. Said to 'crown the day's demonstration with its volume of flame', it 'burnt to the satisfaction of admiring thousands.' The stack was so enormous that the corporation hired nearly sixty stewards (police, fire brigade and public) to completely encircle it, in order to keep the thousands of attendees well back from the flames, sparks, and floating embers, especially children and those adults who had celebrated the royal nuptials by spending the entire day boozing.

Ann Stace probably took her children to the bonfire early on; George and his father went together about 10pm. Being slightly tipsy, George wandered too close to the fire and, after ignoring a verbal warning, he was pulled back to safety by Superintendent Glenister, who said he would 'lock him up' if he didn't behave. William led his son away, and an hour later Glenister met the pair near George's flat. Wishing him a hearty goodnight, the genial superintendent shook George's hand and left.

Father and son walked to William's house in West Street, but George said he needed to speak again to Glenister. At 11.20pm they called at the police station but, finding him absent, George asked Sergeant Ginner to lock him up. Ginner was used to dealing with drunks, especially on high days and holidays, so he told George to go and sleep it off at his father's house. On the way back to West Street George suddenly ran off. William thought he may have returned to the bonfire, so made his way there. It was quarter to midnight and the fire, though mostly burned out, still raged at the heart of its base. The stewards had left, but a number of spectators still hung about, and William heard one of them shouting for help.

According to *The Era,* after uttering 'a few incoherent words' George Stace had dashed into the blazing pile and rolled about in the flames. His feet were close to the edge, so Eddie Shoesmith and Gilbert Thorpe grabbed one each and dragged him out. Eddie stumbled and fell over backwards, losing his grip on George, who stood up and stripped off his burned outer clothes. To the renewed horror of his rescuers, he then ran back into the centre of the fire! This time he was completely engulfed and nobody could safely reach any part of him. Whilst Gilbert ran to the Angel Inn on the corner of St Mary's Terrace to fetch assistance, George rolled himself out of the fire and lay on the scorched earth, almost naked, his skin charred so severely that nobody dared to touch him.

The organisers had left a large, empty wooden box nearby, so Charlie Picknell and four other men lifted poor George onto it and carried him with great care to the infirmary at White Rock. Frederick Ticehurst was called from his bed and George told him that he had run into the fire 'on purpose'. Seeing the extreme burns all over his body Ticehurst knew there was no hope of survival and went home to bed, leaving him in the care of the matron. After expressing gratitude towards everyone who had helped him, George died at 7.30am.

The inquest was held by Coroner Robert Growse. After hearing from the witnesses, the jury concluded that George had committed suicide 'while in a state of temporary insanity'. 'There can be no doubt', wrote *The Era,* 'that he was suffering from delirium produced by intoxication.'

George's gruesome demise was reported in the press all over the UK. From Edinburgh to Bristol, from Belfast to Leeds, readers learned of the 'frightful occurrence' in which a Hastings businessman had 'roasted himself alive'. One reporter remarked that the ghastly incident had 'cast a terrible gloom over the otherwise joyous proceedings of the day'.

The loss of her husband left Ann Stace with six children under fourteen and one on the way. The support of the entire family now fell to her alone. She may have already helped in the shop, but she needed to make herself conversant with every aspect of George's trade, such as how to buy, handle, store, prepare and sell fish, oysters, poultry and game. She was almost certainly the first woman in Hastings to obtain a licence to deal in game.

Under Ann's ownership the business thrived. As the town grew the shop became ever busier and and, and as each of her children reached their teens they would work in the shop. As she prospered, Ann moved the family out of the

DIGRESSION: FEMALE SHOPKEEPERS

Hastings women have sold fish and shellfish for centuries, and in 1826 it was noted that three-quarters of the town's fishmongers were the female relatives of local fishermen. Most of them had stalls and barrows rather than shops. Women shopkeepers were also numerous in Hastings; indeed, by the 1860s almost 40% of shops were in female hands. These were almost all in typical female areas: millinery, staymaking, toy selling and grocery. Women only acquired businesses in male trades by taking over from their late husbands.

It is noteworthy that, whilst men would not hire or apprentice a woman into a male trade, nobody could stop a widow from continuing her late husband's business. This is how Hastings came to have women in trades such as butcher, blacksmith, cabinetmaker, undertaker, plumber, glazier, painter and fly proprietor. If the work required skills that a woman could not acquire, she would hire a trained man, as blacksmith Harriot Ranger did. In contrast, Hannah Morton ran her late husband's High Street china and glass business herself, and when Charlotte Osborne's husband, a printer, died in 1861, she carried on his trade for many years, employing her son as compositor.

Hastings Museum holds two of Mrs Morton's receipts, beautifully illustrated with an etching of the Crystal Palace, and also Mrs Osborne's printing press, which is labelled with only her husband's name.

maisonette above the shop and into a bow-fronted Georgian house at nearby 7 Pelham Place.

In 1867 Ann drew considerable attention to her shop by exhibiting in her front window 'a fine wild swan, which was shot on Pett Level...The bird measures 8ft across from the tips of the wing, and weighs 23lbs'.

Just nine years after George's death, in 1872 Ann Stace died in the infirmary at White Rock after undergoing an operation for a long-standing cancer. She was just forty-five. Her death certificate hid her achievement by recording her occupation as 'Widow of George Stace, poulterer master'. The *HSLO*, under the headline 'Respect to the dead', reported that 'Several of the shops in Castle-street and along the route to High-street were closed as the remains of the late Mrs Stace were being carried to the Cemetery'.

The business was continued by Ann's son George, who moved back into 7 Pelham Place with his family. History repeated itself when he died young in 1881, leaving his wife Mary Ann with children aged five and three and a newborn. Like her mother-in-law, she took over the business and obtained a game licence. When George's executors auctioned the freehold she went along and bid £1,630 (£163,000 today). As her name was announced as the winner the auction room was filled with loud applause.

After four years of juggling childcare and running a busy shop, Mary Ann Stace contracted tuberculosis and died at home in 1885, aged just thirty-four. Again a woman's profession and status were hidden when, on her death certificate, the registrar omitted any reference to her being a business owner, and called her: 'the widow of George Stace, fishmonger master'.

No. 7 Pelham Place is the fourth house along, facing the sea, opposite the Russian gun captured during the Crimean War. The building still exists and is the first house to the west of the former Empire Theatre of Varieties (built in 1899). The ground floor is now part of Playland, and the upper floors are flats. This engraving, by Newman, dates from the 1860s.

References: *HSLO* 12 February 1867 & 5 October 1872; *Sussex Advertiser* 17 March 1863; *Brighton Gazette* 19 March 1863; *The Era* 15 March 1863.

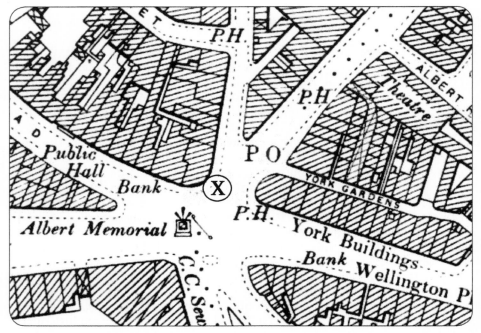

This 1873 street plan shows the location of the Post Office. The X marks the spot outside 4 Bank Buildings where Caroline was hit.

This photograph, taken about 1910, shows (far right) the location of the Post Office in Meadow Road, now called Queen's Road. The Halifax currently occupies the site. The lamp standard on the far left, close to the camera, is outside 4 Bank Buildings.

1871

KILPY'S STICK

BANK BUILDINGS

Caroline Spicer was born in Kent in 1861, just before her parents moved to Hastings. Her father was a railway guard, and the family lived amongst his colleagues in a rented terraced house at 15 Station Road.[1] By the age of ten the narrow confines of Caroline's future were already delineated. After a basic schooling in the bare necessities of reading, writing, arithmetic and needlework, at fourteen she would enter domestic service or perhaps work in a shop. After a few years of low-paid drudgery she would marry and begin a lifetime of unpaid drudgery. Her future could be predicted fairly accurately because her sex and her social class severely limited her life possibilities.

Charles Kilpin's beginnings could not have been more different. From the moment of his birth he was instantly bestowed with privilege. As the son of a wealthy landed proprietor, he received an expensive private education, automatic entry to Oxford University, and was accepted into Gray's Inn to study for the Bar. Being in receipt of an unearned income of £1,600 a year (about £160,000 today) he saw no reason to bother studying for a career, preferring instead to devote himself to a life of sheer self-indulgence.

Kilpin squandered so much money that he ate into his capital, and by 1850 his yearly income had plummeted to just £150 (£15,000 today). 'Although his means were small, he continued those tastes that had been his ruin', explained one reporter. 'He became acquainted with loose characters, whom he met in public houses'. Not only did he gamble heavily at whist, but also he 'led a very dissolute life' and consorted with young men, including a soldier in the Light Dragoons, whom he paid for 'companionship'.

When his elder brother died in 1854 Kilpin inherited his fortune, which multiplied his yearly income tenfold. Despite his excellent academic education he lacked street wisdom. Sentencing a man to six years for blackmailing Kilpin by threatening to expose him for committing an 'unnatural offence' with another man, a judge remarked that Kilpin's wealth made him 'the mark of those who felt anxious to share his property, and who seemed to have made him their prey'.

Kilpin had a curious 'hobby'. When a cute young working man — such as a groom or a waiter — caught his fancy he would impress him by instructing a tailor to make the lad a bespoke suit costing £4–£6 (£400 to £600 today) as a gift. The trouble was, he did not pay the invoice. The tailors extended credit to

1. Clarks shoe shop now occupies the site.

him only because they thought him a gentleman, but he abused his position and their trust and put them through the hassle of suing him to get paid.

As he reached middle age Kilpin would spend winter in London, where his home was 55 Piccadilly, a swanky Mayfair address, whilst the warmer months found him in Hastings or St Leonards, where he stayed in lodging houses.

In London in October 1870 a policeman reprehended him for marching along, 'pushing females off the pavement'. He retorted haughtily that he would 'do as he liked', and, moreover, that he 'must have room to walk!' As if to punctuate his assertion he struck a random lad on the head and thumped a passing pedestrian, inflicting a severe blow to her breast. He was arrested and charged with being being drunk and disorderly. At his police court hearing (which was attended by a member of the Associate Institute for Improving and Enforcing the Laws for the Protection of Women) the magistrate ordered Kilpin to pay the poor woman compensation. He also remarked that Kilpin's conduct towards innocent strangers was 'so thoroughly brutal' that it brought his sanity into question. If he were sane, he would serve three months in prison.

Seven months later Kilpin was lodging at St Michael's Place, Hastings. He was well known in town as a figure of fun: a common drunkard, and yet attired in a gentleman's bespoke suits and silk top hats.

About 6pm on 19th May 1871 ten-year-old Caroline Spicer was about to cross the road from Bank Buildings to the Post Office on Meadow Road. She walked behind 'Kilpy', as locals called him, as he swaggered along in his entitled, arrogant fashion. With reckless abandon he swung his walking stick behind him, striking young Caroline a heavy blow to the shoulder. The impact thrust her backward, causing her head to collide with an iron street lamp. Seemingly oblivious to his actions, Kilpin continued striding boldly along. The incident happened directly outside 4 Bank Buildings (now Subway), the premises of thirty-eight-year-old auctioneer Henry Tidy Develin. As he went to help Caroline she stood up, rubbed her head, began to weep, and walked away.

For the next few days Caroline suffered pains in her head and ears, felt drowsy, struggled to stay awake, and experienced bouts of nausea, even vomiting occasionally. 'Kilpy knocked me down and hurt my poor head', she sobbed to her mother. 'Why did he do it? I have never done him any harm'.

Mrs Spicer twice took Caroline to the free clinic at the infirmary. She was examined by Dr Trollope on 29th May and by Dr Hubert Braye on 31st. Each time she was given a bottle of medicine and sent home, where on 8th June she died. Dr Braye gave the cause of death as 'concussion, epilepsy and typhoid'. His post mortem showed 'great brain mischief': a softening and inflammation arising from being struck a blow.

Coroner Sheppard held an inquest on 12th June at the Clarence Hotel, Station Road. After hearing the evidence, the jurymen asked for time to consider their verdict. They were conducted to a private room and the coroner's officer was sworn to keep them in complete isolation. Kilpin had to wait anxiously to find out if he was going to be charged with manslaughter.

John Spicer	Head.	mar	40		Railway Guard.
Harriet D?	Wife	mar		45	
Emily D?	Daur			11	Scholar.
Caroline D?	Daur.			10	D?
William D?	Son		7		D?
Alice D?	Daur.			3	
Anne D?	Daur.			2	

The 1871 census for 15 Station Road, listing John and Harriet Spicer and their five children. It was taken on 2nd April, and just a few weeks later Caroline would be dead.

When the jury finally emerged the foreman said that they had decided on 'accidental death'. However, they wanted Kilpin to be formally reprimanded for his appalling conduct. Mr Sheppard duly obliged. He told Kilpin most firmly that he was 'morally responsible' for Caroline's death and should 'give up those habits of intoxication which were a disgrace to him and the education he had received'. Kilpin made no reply but a reporter remarked that he 'looked repentant enough as he listened with the tears trickling down his cheeks to the solemn and expressive words of the Coroner', adding that 'resolution will be of little avail in a wrestle with the Devil Alcohol.'

Kilpin was not yet out of the woods. On 19th June he was brought up in front of magistrates Edward Hayles and Robert Deudney, accompanied by his expensive London solicitor, Mr Philbrick, of Garrard & James of Pall Mall, on a charge of 'killing and slaying' Caroline Spicer. Mr Norris, prosecuting, said that if Kilpin had the 'common and decent feelings of a man', he would have 'turned back and picked her up'.

During a three-day adjournment, Kilpin was held in a police cell, a far cry from his usual five-star accommodation. Upon resumption it was time for his fancy solicitor to earn his fat fee. Painting his client as the helpless victim of an addiction to which he would 'remain a slave for the rest of his life', he begged the justices to spare Kilpin the 'expense and anxiety' of a trial at the assizes and offered to pay compensation to the Spicers to avoid it. The unlucky couple had already lost two of their ten children in infancy and another at age seven. Caroline's death left them devastated.

The editor of the *HSLO* called Kilpin a gentleman who had fallen to 'the lowest depths of degradation'; he was 'the pot-house companion of the drunken and vicious, the terror of the nervous, the laughing-stock of children and adults'. If the 'miserable man...has any moral consciousness left the thought must haunt him through life that whether the blow was given deliberately or accidentally an inoffensive child met her death at his hand.'

The magistrates sent Kilpin to trial at the assizes, where he was found not guilty of manslaughter. However, his family paid all the Spicer's out-of-pocket expenses and in addition gave them a 'present' of £20 (£2,000 today) for the loss of their child. The judge expressed his approval, adding that they should also ensure he did not walk the streets whilst drunk.

The *HSLO* approved of the verdict. Its editor remarked that Kilpin's 'habits of intoxication' had made him 'the mockery of one portion of the community and the disgust of the other'. He should leave Hastings at once and never return, because 'for evermore his name must be associated with the death of this unfortunate child.'

Sadly, even killing a child did not prompt Kilpin to cease his inebriated street swaggering. Less than two years later the *HSLO,* in a report headed 'Kilpin redivivus' (i.e. reborn) revealed that P.C. Noakes had spotted him in the street, 'drunk, swinging his stick, and frightening ladies and children off the pavement'. He ignored the summons and did not bother to attend Hastings Police Court, where he was fined 10s (worth £50 today) in his absence. On being informed that Kilpin had crossed the Channel, the magistrate remarked that he 'wished the French Republic joy of him'.

Kilpin died four years later, aged sixty-six. He left £12,000 (worth about £1.2m today). The chief beneficiary was his late brother's grandson, but he also left a bequest to 'institutions for the reformation of unfortunate females [prostitutes] in the Metropolis'.

Despite all the terrible things Charles Kilpin had done in his life that dragged his good family name into the gutter, and regardless of his having killed a little girl, he was not outcast from his kin; his body was taken back to Kingsclere in Hampshire, where it was interred in the family vault.

References: *Oxford University Herald* 15 March 1856; *Worcester Journal* 14 March 1857; *Morning Post* 29 October 1870; *HSLO* 17 & 24 June, 15 & 22 July 1871 and 19 April 1873.

1877

The Cruel Sea

Rock-a-Nore

Paraphrased from the *Hastings & St Leonards Observer*, 6 January 1877.

Early on Monday 1st January a gale, terrific in force and fearfully disastrous in its effects, burst in upon this town. Up till about six o'clock the morning was fine, the wind moderate, the sea calm. Shortly after that time, however, a gale sprung up, increasing as the tide grew stronger, until between nine and ten o'clock it had attained an intensity of fury which, with the huge volume of waters in the Channel, threatened destruction.

High water was at 1150, and it was with feelings of the greatest alarm that hundreds of dwellers on the seafront watched the gale speed on, destruction borne in upon every wave, the disaster of one moment looking likely to be surpassed by still more terrible disasters. At ten o'clock a diminution in the force of the storm was perceptible, and as the time for high water approached it became evident that the worst was over; that the huge waves which rushed in upon the parade breaking their mighty volumes with a thundering roar, had lost their most potent ally, for the winds that for hours previously had lashed them so fiercely were now subsiding. People could breathe a sigh of relief.

But disastrous enough were its effect, as the *debris* strewed around on all sides made but too plainly evident. Private property had sustained very heavy losses, but the greater part of the destruction was to be seen in the wreckage of the property of the Local Board. The amount of damage done will cost several thousand pounds to make good.

Throughout the raging of the gale, the streets were impassible, but wherever some of the effects of the storm could be watched crowds assembled, and it need hardly be said that the spectacle, sad as it was in some places, was not without many touches of grim humour arising out of an unsolicited acquaintance of some of the spectators with the spray of the waves as they dashed in, or the rivers which some of the more venturesome occasionally attempted to ford.

When the storm had abated the principal thoroughfares continued to be thronged, especially the front line, along which streamed whole crowds from east to west. During the afternoon and even after nightfall the *debris* in many places attracted the curious and the anxious.

WEST MARINA.

The ravages were greater here than in almost any other part of the borough, and when the tide retired, it left behind a pitiable scene. The massive balustrades in front of the houses were, in the majority of cases, forced completely in by the weight and violence of the water, and huge masses of masonry hurled into the areas below, or scattered about on the pavement and in the road. Steps were torn up, iron railings were bent and twisted and contorted in every imaginable form and shape. There were numerous instances in which doors, bolted, barred, and barricaded, had been forced bodily in, and through these openings the sea at once poured in one seething fierce torrent, deluging the bottoms of the houses and committing fearful havoc. The furniture of the rooms flooded was either broken up or floated out to sea. The scene of ruin and desolation is heart-rending in the extreme. The distress of some of the occupants of the houses was most lamentable.

The storm here caused almost as much destruction as if some mighty enemy had swooped suddenly upon the place and laid it waste. The waves, carrying tons of beach on their bosom, swept in; iron railings were broken down, solid masonry overturned and destroyed, windows and doors beaten in as if they were so much cardboard, business establishments and houses completely swamped, gutted, and ruined. Far away still westward, it was evident the waves had rolled with irresistible force, carrying everything that lay in their way on their onward march of destructiveness. The railway lines were not only flooded, but in places torn up and rendered useless for locomotion, and the railway traffic from Pevensey had to be entirely suspended.

The shop of Mr Moon, grocer, was quite gutted. A tremendous wave rushed against the house, hurled the strongly-barricaded door off its hinges, and the beach, stones, crystalized fruits, biscuits, and sweets were mixed up in inextricable confusion.

In many of the houses there was as much as ten and twelve feet of water in the basement rooms. Floating about on the surface one could see every description of household furniture, chairs, bedsteads, crockeryware, and small nic-nacs that had adorned, perhaps, the mantelshelf or sideboard. Upwards of thirty houses have been handled in this rough and merciless fashion. It was a scene, in all truth, of the most complete and heartrending destruction; and the whole locality reminded one forcibly of a town that had been sacked and plundered by the fierce soldiery of a foreign army.

The parade wall has been almost entirely destroyed. The stone facing has been washed away, whilst the clayey soil of which the parade is chiefly composed has almost completely disappeared under the action of the sea. The iron railing separating the roadway from the parade was almost entirely demolished, the iron bars being doubled and twisted like pieces of ribbon into every imaginable shape. In one or two instances, ponderous pieces of railing were carried by the waves for a distance of many yards, and were seen half-embedded in the road, while large stones of considerable weight lay spread about in all directions. They were lifted by the waves like so many pebbles, and flung in many instances with fearful violence against the fronts of the houses.

The greater portion of the earth that had been tipped on the beach near the old St Leonards Church, as a preliminary step towards the widening of the parade, has been washed away by the sea. The clay was washed up in large quantities on the parade itself, and rendered it at places almost impassable to pedestrians, unless they did not mind wallowing up to their knees in mire. Even where the road and parade are much wider, the sea made a complete breach over both, and, following over into the areas, got into the basements of the houses. This is an occurrence that has never been known to have taken place before, and it speaks volumes for the alarming violence and height of the tide.

In the afternoon the Marina presented a scene of unusual bustle and turmoil. Crowds of pedestrians on their way to view the ruin and havoc lined the parade and pavement, whilst the roadway was almost blocked with carriages passing backwards and forwards. Carpenters and others were engaged in putting up barricades and erecting additional defences, whilst vans were standing at the doors of the houses being loaded with furniture. Everyone was busy, and notwithstanding the calamity that had befallen them, the people went about their work in an earnest and cheerful manner.

What will be done to aid the sufferers, of course, is a question of the future. That many persons who can ill afford the loss have lost their all is but too patent. We may, however, be assured that something will be done, if not to entirely heal their wounds, at least to alleviate their sufferings. The residents and visitors of Hastings and St Leonards can be generous when occasion is shown for generosity.

CAVES ROAD.

A vast volume of water rushed round the corner of Caves-road, flooding that road and the Market to a considerable depth, and penetrating into many of the houses. The road was flooded with water to a depth of two or three feet, and many of the houses were inundated.

Between twelve and one o'clock, without scarcely a warning, huge pieces of cliff fell, and for a considerable distance the road was blocked up with thousands of tons of rock and earth that had thus fallen. Caves-cottages had a very narrow escape from being utterly destroyed by this avalanche. Doors were forced in, and ceilings fell partially through, and it is almost a miracle that the cottages and their inmates were not involved in one common ruin. Fortunately, when the cliff was seen to be toppling and giving way, an alarm was immediately raised, and everyone was got out. The cliff is still in a very dangerous state and large masses of it may become detached at any moment.

EVERSFIELD-PLACE.

The waves played with tremendous fury on the sea defences, and at intervals the surface of the parade was very much broken. An immense quantity of beach was thrown up, covering both the road and parade to a considerable depth — in fact, in some places the shingle was so thick that only the tops of the rails could be seen. The covered seat stationed in the centre of the parade was completely smashed and broken up, and the *debris* strewed over the roadway and parade.

THE PIER.

The iron grating at the entrance was completely washed from its foundations, whilst the east toll-house was shifted from its position. At the end several of the gas lamps were torn away from the deck by the fury of the waves, as was also the flagstaff at the south end. Part of the iron railing from the Pier to the Baths has been washed away, and the flag-stones thrown bodily from their proper position, in some cases nearly to the centre of the road. The head of the Pier is a complete wreck.

WHITE ROCK.

When the storm was at its height, the scene was grand and beautiful. Huge columns of water and white flecked foam rising majestically in the air and precipitating themselves with tremendous force on the parade and road, and even deluging the fronts of the houses. A huge baulk of timber was swept up and flung with irresistible force against the iron railing protecting the wall. The sea made a breach right across the road, and for a long time rendered it impassable both to carriages and pedestrians.

Whilst the tide was flowing many amusing incidents were witnessed here, and ample food for merriment afforded the crowd of persons assembled at the corner of Robertson-street. Several adventuresome, reckless individuals in attempting to pass along the front speedily came to grief, and found themselves drenched to the skin by the volumes of water which surged over the parade and rushed against the fronts of the houses.

At the Seaside Hotel great difficulty was experienced in keeping out the seawater and a gang of men was busily engaged behind the defences that had been erected in sweeping away and baling out the water that was constantly rushing in. At one time, when the sea was just commencing to pour over the parade in earnest, an unusually high wave swept right against the hotel and took several men who were working with their brooms in front, and also a lady, off their legs, and drenched them to the skin, to the no small amusement of the assembled spectators.

A sketch of the land end of the pier, by J. Greenaway, published in the *Illustrated London News* 20 January 1877.

Huge banks of timber, carried off from the Aquarium works, could be seen borne in upon the waves. Indeed, Castle-street may be said to have been one mass of wreckage from the Aquarium.

THE TOWN CENTRE.

On Carlisle-parade the waters rose to a height and extended to a distance never attained in any preceding gale. In immense volumes the water rushed up by the Queen's Hotel, through Harold-place, and burst in literally foam-crested waves away into the Queen's-road, with the force of a river from the hills, flooding Bank-buildings, Middle-street, Queen's-road, a portion of Wellington-place, and the lower extremity of Havelock-road. The Albert Memorial was the centre of a scene of confusion, excitement, and alarm. Waves swept through the streets, and the inundation assumed the most alarming dimension. In some places men were up to their waists in water, and so strong was the rush of the current that it was almost impossible to keep on one's legs. The boatmen were, however, fully prepared for the emergency. Pleasure crafts of every description had been drawn up into Robertson-street, and along Queen's-road, safe from the clutches of the devouring aqueous element.

The scene presented was one which would never be erased from the memory. Crowds of spectators, amongst whom were a good sprinkling of the fair sex, were gathered at every point of rising ground to be found in the immediate locality, with the torrent of water at their feet rushing by with a defiant roar; men in complete suits of oilskin were plunging about in the water, picking up and stopping the baulks of timber and other *debris* and wreckage washed in; small youths, with a triumphant grin on their face, were wading about almost up to their armpits, in a state of frantic enjoyment.

Assistants in the various business establishments were standing behind their barricades with coats off and short sleeves and trousers tucked up, baling out and sweeping away the water that was every minute surging over the tops of their defences. Traffic was almost entirely stopped. It was only with the greatest difficulty that vehicles could be drawn across the road, the roaring torrent of water naturally frightening the horses, who but for the precautions taken would probably have started off, and occasioned serious damage if not loss of life, considering the thronged state of the thoroughfare.

The Cricket Ground was flooded all over to a considerable depth, and the whole neighbourhood was nothing but one vast, unbroken sheet of water.

GEORGE-STREET.

The sea flowed through West-street and into George-street, flooding the dwelling houses of the poorer class who inhabit that part of the borough. The shop-keepers in George-street had barricaded their doorways; but, notwithstanding this, several shops and cellars were flooded. The cellars of the Anchor Inn were filled with water, as were those of several of the beer-houses in West-street.

Some of the boat-houses and workshops were considerably knocked about. At Mr Tutt's boat-shed the portion which faces the sea was completely battered in, and the ground-work round the foundations of the houses was washed away. At a shed in the occupation of Mr Tapp, blacksmith, there was an awful smash. The forge was greatly damaged by the beach which was thrown on it, and the water which flooded the place.

In Breeds-place the basements were completely flooded, and in Caroline-place and Beach cottages the distressing sights of flooded houses, of ruined property, and of wailing women and weeping children were renewed, with many sympathizing hearts and ready hands ministering, regardless of their own comfort or safety, to the necessities of the unfortunate victims. Over these houses the gigantic waves rose and swept, dashing in windows, breaking in doors, and taking a possession against which there could be no dispute.

Westward of Breeds-place the trail of the gale was traced in great destruction. The sea-wall was broken down in places; the sea had rushed over its ordinary boundaries with such terrible force and volume that iron palings were torn up, huge stones were lifted up, woodwork was snapped asunder and broken up as though it had been so much match-boarding. Holes, deep and broad, were dug out in places on the parade, as if some excavators had been employed there with pick and shovel.

FATAL ACCIDENT.

A life has been sacrificed, one human victim has been swept into eternity by the merciless storm — one poor man, who mayhap but a few hours previous was wishing to and receiving from friends expressions of 'Many happy New Years', had been beaten down on this New Year's Day, and was lying cold in death at the infirmary.

It happened by the mortuary which was being erected in Rock-a-Nore Road. Two bricklayers, William Oak and Charles Croft, working for the local Board, were at work together in a building near the lifeboat house. It was an old mill, about to be used as a gun shed by the Royal Naval Artillery Volunteers.

Nearby William Pont, a sailmaker, was working indoors on a small yacht called the *Foam.* The storm caused the sea to burst in the door, and he asked William and Charles to fasten it. This was not part of their duty; they did it as a favour. Whilst they were doing so, suddenly a heavy wave came towards them, floated the boats which were stored in the building and swept through. William was knocked down and the *Foam*, propelled by the wave, whacked Charles in the back and crushed him against a wall. As the wave receded William recovered himself and called out to Charles, who replied, 'I can't get up!' With the assistance of Mr Pont William carried Charles outside. He was bleeding a good deal. He fainted, but recovered and remained conscious whilst being conveyed to the infirmary. The road along the seafront being impassable they carried him up onto the West Hill, down Wallinger's Walk, up Cambridge Road then around by St Michael's Place and down the steep incline to the rear of the infirmary. Here he was placed under the care of Mrs Caroline Lane, the matron and head of the establishment.

Dr Augustus Ticehurst examined Charles, and found he had sustained a severe internal injury: a large splinter of timber had penetrated the lower part of his back, leaving a wound so large it could admit three fingers. The passage to the bladder was torn and other parts of the stomach ruptured. A few hours later, the poor man died in excruciating agony.

An inquest was held at the infirmary by Dr Ticehurst's father, Frederick, the coroner at the time. It was established that Charles Croft was a fifty-eight-year-old widower, originally from Brightling, who had lived for many years at Old London Road. The jury returned a verdict of 'accidental death', there being no one to blame but the cruel sea.

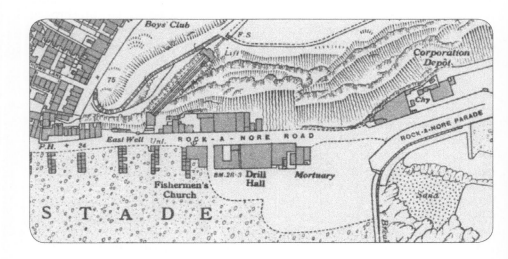

BELFRY BLUES

CHURCH ROAD

James Corney was born in Brighton at the end of 1831; his father was a wheelwright in the coach building trade and James, the only boy of seven children, moved to Hastings, where he apprenticed as a coach joiner at the famous carriage building firm of Rock & Son at White Rock.

Amelia Hayward was born in Hastings in 1836. Her father Esau abandoned his wife and three small girls before Amelia, the eldest, had reached her third birthday. Left penniless and destitute, her mother begged money of the All Saints' parish overseers, who refused to help and passed the burden to her birth parish, St Mary-in-the-Castle. A year later Esau appeared in the London newspapers: he had stolen a cheque for a vast sum from his employer, a butcher in Aldgate. Tried at the Old Bailey, he served six months in Newgate and then emigrated to Tasmania, where he married bigamously and started a new family. His first wife knew nothing of his whereabouts, and supported her daughters by opening a greengrocer shop at 53 High Street. All three girls learned useful trades; Amelia became a dressmaker.

Amelia married James Corney in 1860 and by 1872 she had produced five daughters and a son. James, a deeply religious man, followed his true vocation when he left Rock & Son in 1868 in order to work at the newly built St Paul's church, on the corner of Church Road and Ellenslea Road. Initially its vestry clerk,[1] James later became its verger,[2] and an enthusiastic singer in its excellent, fifty-strong choir.

James rented the upper part of a five-storey house at 6 Blomfield Terrace, a minute's walk from the church. In the autumn of 1876 Amelia fell down a flight of stairs and damaged her spine. After a few weeks of suffering she died of her injuries, aged just forty. James was left to raise the six children, aged between fifteen and four, and engaged an old family friend as nanny-housekeeper to look after them whilst he was at work.

Among the many wealthy patrons of St Paul's were the local MP Thomas Brassey and his wife, Annie. After travelling 36,000 miles — and circumnavigating the globe — in their yacht the *Sunbeam*, they arrived back at Hastings on 26th May 1877. Mrs Brassey's first priority (after snatching a few hours sleep) was to go in her private carriage to the early communion at St Paul's.[3]

1. The clerk or secretary of the parish vestry records minutes of the vestry meetings.
2. A lay minister who assists the clergy in the conduct of public worship.
3. Annie Brassey wrote several fascinating books about her voyages on the family yacht.

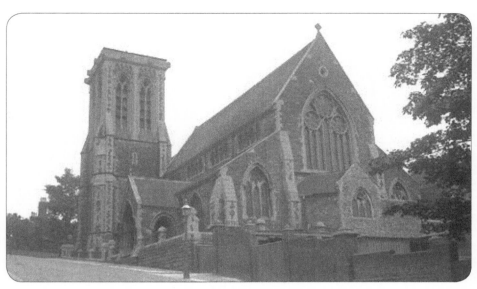

St Paul's from Ellenslea Road.

The church from outside the rectory in Church Road.

Designed in pseudo decorated gothic, St Paul's cost nearly £26,000 (£2.6m today), paid for entirely by multi-millionaire William Gilliat of East Hoathly, whose wealth derived from his tobacco plantations in Richmond, Virginia, where the workforce included Black slaves. He died in 1868, before the church opened, but was commemorated in a large brass plaque above the marble font. In 1865 his daughter had married Irish-born British Army chaplain Henry Robinson MA, and so, of course, he became St Paul's first rector. The Robinsons lived opposite the church at The Priory, a splendid, twelve-bedroomed mansion in an acre of grounds, where they were looked after by seven residential servants.

The exterior of the church was of local blue stone with Bath stone dressings, whilst the highly ornate interior boasted ninety-three solid marble columns and a wealth of stained glass, stone tracery, alabaster and brass. It consisted of a nave and two side aisles, the northern one leading to a square bell tower 82ft high. Reminiscent of a Venetian campanile, it was visible for miles around. A planned 80ft spire was never added, but a magnificent organ was designed and installed and the highly talented organist, musical director and choir master Dr Abram ensured that St Paul's quickly gained fame as a centre of musical excellence.

On consecration day in 1869 the rector treated 180 well-off ladies and gentlemen to a banquet lunch. It quickly became the favourite church of the fashionable and the wealthy, as well as their servants. The famous novelist Sheila Kaye-Smith was married there in 1924. Forty years later the church was demolished — 'a most grievous loss' — and the beautiful rectory was bulldozed. Both sites are now covered by modern but soulless blocks of flats.

Two weeks later, on Friday 8th June, his daughter Annie's sixteenth birthday, James left home to perform his daily task of tolling the church bell at 8am. He usually popped home in between his church duties, but that day none of his children saw him. When he failed to return after the 5.30pm service Emma, who was fourteen, and a younger sister went to St Paul's to find him.[4]

After looking around in vain, and becoming increasingly anxious, they were relieved to spot his hat on its usual peg in the vestry. They entered the bell tower and passed up the steps to the bell-room, where they were faced with the horrific sight of their father suspended by his neck from a rope, limp and lifeless, his feet not touching the floor.

The younger girl ran out screaming to the curate, who called out to a couple of painters working on a nearby house, saying there had been an accident and asking if they could assist. They immediately cut James's body down, but it was too late: his corpse was stone cold.

A young doctor, Henry Humphreys,[5] fetched from his home at nearby 9 Magdalen Terrace, judged that James had been dead for about eight hours. P.C. Noakes was also summoned, and together they examined the scene and questioned Emma and the painters. The body had been found hanging by a thick rope, 30ft long, which was used to hoist the Union Flag up to the top of the tower. A ladder had been placed against one wall of the belfry, and James must have climbed it, tied the rope around his neck and jumped off.

The inquest was held the following evening at Campbell's Hotel, 1 St John's Road[6] by Charles Davenport Jones. Dr John Abram, the organist of St Paul's, was foreman of the jury. The chief witness, Emma, explained that, since her mother died, her father had 'grieved a good deal' and suffered from insomnia. The verdict of the jury was 'suicide whilst in an unsound state of mind'.

The editor of the *HSLO* called the incident 'one of the saddest and most distressing cases of suicide that we have had to record'. James was 'a cheerful man, of a most obliging and courteous disposition'. Lately he had 'looked gloomy and downcast, but no one for a moment thought that he would make off with himself'. The affair 'occasioned painful excitement in the neighbourhood for he was universally esteemed.' Those who knew James spoke of him as a 'kind-hearted, frank-souled, genial man',

> And yet, alas! who can control his fate who, that exults in the strength of his intellect to-day, shall say that the morrow may not see him helpless as a child, his reason overturned, all things distorted in his view, beauty transformed into ugliness, pleasure into pain, and the only relief left a mad leap into that terrible void, that awful unknown,

4. She is not named in any report but was probably Fanny, twelve or Kate, ten.
5. In the 1880s he gained a local reputation as a public speaker on the benefits of vegetarianism and temperance, and accompanied Dr Elizabeth Blackwell to women's suffrage meetings.
6. Owned and run by Mary Campbell, who took over the licence after her husband's death. It still stands and is now called The Royal.

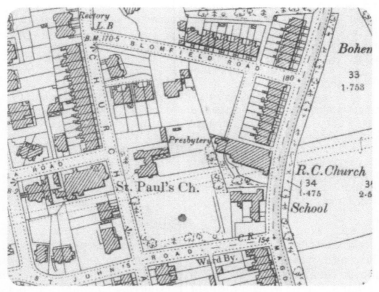

Map showing Blomfield Terrace (now Road), St Paul's, and,
opposite the church, The Priory and its grounds.

The contents of James Corney's house were listed for sale in the
Sussex Advertiser on 19 June 1877, just ten days after he died.

NO. 6, BLOMFIELD TERRACE, ST. LEONARDS-ON-SEA.

SALE OF CAPITAL MODERN HOUSEHOLD FURNITURE, LINEN, CHINA, GLASS, AND EFFECTS.

Mr. Bridger

IS instructed to SELL BY AUCTION, on the above premises, on FRIDAY, June 22nd, 1877, at One o'clock punctually, the whole of the useful modern HOUSEHOLD FURNITURE, comprising a Spanish mahogany cellaret sideboard, chairs, couches, and tables, dinner waggons, engravings, fenders, fireirons, pardonians.

HANDSOME CHIMNEY GLASSES, Brussels carpets nearly new, rugs, wool mats, lustres, clocks, parian marble figures, under glass shades, walnut-wood spring-seated DRAWING ROOM SUITE, covered in green rep, centre and side tables, whatnots, gas fittings, chiffonier, barometer, floorcloth, ball table, chairs.

BEDROOM APPOINTMENTS consist of iron and mahogany Arabian bedsteads, feather beds, wool mattress, palliasses, blankets, counterpanes, mahogany and painted chests of drawers, mahogany marble top washstands, china toilet fittings, glasses, dressing tables, towel airers.

Japanned BATHS, LINEN, CHINA, and the usual kitchen requisites.

On View the morning of Sale, and Catalogues may be obtained of the AUCTIONEER, at his Estate Agency Offices, 7, Claremont, Hastings.

on the brink of which all stand, but from which all sane men shrink? But who can speak ill of the late verger, done to death by his own hand? While he had troops of friends, he never had an enemy. He was a hard-working and humble official, but, assuredly, no ordinary man to draw words of eloquence like these, as a tribute to his memory, from the Rector:

'All who have at any time worshipped in my church know how his duties were discharged, and subsequently how much they have lost by his departure among us. To me his loss is irreparable; and it is only right, at this most solemn time, to testify to his inestimable worth, his many virtues, above all his truthfulness, his honesty, and his deep religious convictions. From a stranger, he became long since a friend, entirely honoured and trusted by me, and I shall be only too thankful if, in any way, I can repay to the children the debt I owe to their lamented father.'

The two eldest, Annie and Emma, were already training to be schoolteachers, but the rector took charge of the younger ones. He and (especially) his wife were fabulously wealthy and could easily have paid a family to foster the four youngest, or even moved them into the rectory; after all, they had twelve bedrooms and no offspring. Instead he 'repaid his debt' by splitting them up, sending them a great distance away, and asking the congregation to pay for their support.

Fanny, thirteen, went to her relations in Brighton and trained to be a servant. William, four, was separated from his sisters and sent to an orphanage in Wiltshire, making it difficult (if not impossible) for them to visit him. Although there were convents in Sussex Katie, nine, and Mary, seven, were placed in one in Berkshire. The rector gave a 'benefit sermon' in aid of the convent, which raised a whopping £101 11s 6d (over £100k today) towards the girls' upkeep, but just three years later the Sisters of Mercy asked him for more money. A year later the benevolent reverend told a reporter that he had visited the children, and let them stay in his mansion at Christmas before sending them back to their far-away orphanages.

It was pleasing to discover that as adults they chose to return to Hastings: William trained to be a compositor on a local newspaper, Katie became a teacher at St Andrew's School and Fanny worked as a lady's maid. In their seventies, Annie, Fanny, Katie and Emma and her husband shared a house at 101 Braybrooke Road.

The Rev Mr Robinson became rector of Westfield in 1881, where he remained until his death in 1888. He was buried in his father-in-law's family vault. In their wills he and his wife left the equivalent of £500k and £1.4m.

References: *HSLO* 12 Sept 1874; 9 & 16 June 1877; *Sussex Agricultural Express* 12 June 1877; *Sussex Advertiser* 13 June 1877. Calvin Schermerhorn (2011) *Money Over Mastery, Family Over Freedom: Slavery in the Antebellum Upper South.* p150.

Well Mysterious

Halton Green

Lovers of panto were spoiled for choice in Hastings in the winter of 1881. 'Puss in Boots' was playing at the Music Hall near the Memorial, and at the Pier Pavilion the indefatigable resident entertainment manager Johnny Hunter was staging his company's production of 'Robinson Crusoe and Man Friday'. On offer at the two-year-old Warrior Square Concert Rooms was 'Little Bo Peep', 'a grand new musical supernatural and spectacular comic pantomime' produced by a renowned London theatre troupe.

Twenty-one-year-old Frederick Shoobridge and his girlfriend Annie Newman opted for the latter. The venue was, after all, a mere pebble's throw from 7 Warrior Square Terrace, where Annie, a kitchenmaid, was one of five residential domestic servants looking after millionaire barrister Hugh Dawson, his wife and their two teenage children.[1]

The couple had been 'keeping company' for seven months, were very happy together and had never had a quarrel. Both grew up with fathers who were coachmen; Annie at Silverhill and Fred at 15 Western Road. After serving an apprenticeship as a boot and shoe maker, he had been working for Edward Robinson for eight months. Three weeks earlier he had moved in with Mr Robinson and his wife in the maisonette above the shop at 140 St Andrew's Road, next door to the Fountain Inn.

After work on Tuesday 27th December, Fred went to his parents' house at 8 Stainsby Street for dinner, and then called for Annie in good time to attend the panto, the full title of which was 'Little Bo Peep who lost her sheep, or Harlequin Boy Blue, the Princess Superba, Goldenheart the Good, and Alcohol, the wicked Demon of the universe'. Judging by the review in the *HSLO* the couple had a wonderful time. The paper called it 'a gratifying success...the comic business throughout was admirably sustained, and the roars of laughter and applause were well merited and genuine tokens of the appreciation felt by the delighted audiences. The harlequinade is really good and the pantomimic absurdities were a specially "convulsing" feature.'

1. One of them, sixteen-year-old Charles Dawson, was in adulthood a gentleman archaeologist and the author of an infamous hoax. The Piltdown Man was a paleoanthropological fraud in which bone fragments were presented as the fossilised remains of a previously unknown early human. Although there were suspicions about its authenticity from the start, the discovery was broadly accepted. In 1953 it was shown to be a hoax, and an extensive scientific review in 2016 established that Charles Dawson was its likely perpetrator.

WARRIOR SQUARE CONCERT ROOMS,

and it is to this, therefore, that we first give our attention. Here, commencing this evening at half-past seven, Mr. Henry S. Dacre's celebrated London pantomime company occupy the boards for thirteen nights, during which time they will be engaged in the production of a grand new musical supernatural and spectacular comic pantomime, entitled, "Little Bo Peep who lost her sheep, or Harlequin Boy Blue, the Princess Superba, Goldenheart the Good, and Alcohol, the wicked Demon of the universe." Mr. Dacre is well-known here as the manager of Pink Dominos, Truth, and the Corsican Brothers companies, &c., and the name is sufficient guarantee to the people of these towns of the genuineness of the presentation, and the excellent abilities of the company engaged. Miss Stratherne Hawley, one of the *artistes*, will impersonate one of the necessary adjuncts of a pantomime, and a character that is never omitted, namely, the Good Fairy. Her host of regal advisers are taken by several well-known ladies. Miss Amy Tilley will sustain the title *role*, and Miss Mildenhall, Boy Blue. Mr. J. A. Hybert is engaged for Dame Crump, and patrons of the performances may look for a large amount of fun from that gentleman, and also from Simple Simon (Mr. Goldsworthy). Space does not permit of our enumerating all the various characters, therefore we will pass on to the scenery, which is entirely new, and designed and painted by Mr. W. J. Burton and assistants. The scenes number seven, and the transformation scene will be on a resplendent scale, such as has heretofore never been seen in this town. The grouping of the ballets has been entrusted to Miss McGregor. The costumes are from well-known London firms, and Mr. Hybert has had the arranging of the comic scenes. A juvenile company of pantomimists are engaged, and if report speaks correctly they are simply marvellous. We must leave our readers to patronise the rooms and judge for themselves.

Review of the panto Edward watched on his final night. *HSLO* 31 December 1881.

Mrs Shoobridge sold Robert's goat-chaise and goats in 1884.

The well used to be on a spot that is now at the foot of Egremont Place, between 118 Old London Road and 14 Rotherfield Avenue. It was the only water supply for several dozen houses.

Afterwards Fred walked Annie home and, as they fondly said goodnight at about 11pm, he spotted an acquaintance, Tom Edwards. As Tom lived at 24 Earl Street, the pair walked back to Hastings together. They were full of Christmas revelry and, with the cheerful music of the orchestra still ringing in their ears, Fred whistled happy tunes whilst Tom danced merrily along the streets. It was about midnight when they parted on the corner of South Terrace, just a couple of minutes' walk from their respective homes.

In the bottom corner of the green at Halton, close to a footpath, was a public well, 75ft deep, containing about 4ft of water. Nobody supervised it, and its two wooden hatches might be found open or closed. At a town council meeting in 1873 Cllr Russell warned that it was 'very dangerous', and urged the town clerk to take action. Nothing was done. The subject was raised again on 4th November 1881 by Cllr Bradnam, who requested that a street lamp be placed next to it. Nothing was done. Seven weeks later, on 28th December, local resident George Down was at the well at about 2pm, grappling for pails, when the hooks became caught on something. He managed to pull it to the surface of the water and, judging by the weight, he suspected it was a dead body. He fetched his mate George Leadbetter and a few other men, and with immense difficulty they heaved the corpse 70-odd feet to the surface.

A policeman and a doctor were brought to examine the body and the scene. It was a young man, and it seemed that he had simply fallen in. The corpse was conveyed to the Dun Horse public house at nearby 29 Albion Street to await the coroner's instructions. Nobody who saw the man's face recognised him. Halton was a small community comprising a few streets of modest terraced houses for labouring folk and everyone knew each other. Strangers were rare because Halton had no attractions that might draw outsiders to visit.

By the end of the day Hastings Police had matched the unknown corpse with a young shoemaker who had been reported missing by his employer when he failed to return home after taking his young lady to a pantomime.

The inquest was held at the Halton Working Men's Club.[2] Coroner Charles Davenport Jones and his jury began proceedings by walking along to the Dun Horse to view the body, then spent an hour hearing from witnesses. Tom Edwards, the last person to see Fred alive, said he had been perfectly sober and 'in the best of spirits'. When they parted Fred was yards from home; it was midnight and he was working the next morning. He had mentioned feeling low-spirited of late, because he was worried about his liver, which Dr Julius had said was 'in a consumption'. However, he seemed well when he was whistling cheerily during their amble along the seafront and through the town centre.

Fred's father threw a little light upon the mystery: when Fred was eight they had lived at Halton for a short time; however, they did not have any friends or family in the area, and there was no fathomable reason why Fred would be there, particularly in the pitch black early hours of mid-winter. When his son was ill he had expressed a desire to 'go to sleep and not to wake any more', but since he recovered he had not uttered such sentiments again.

It was a baffling case. Fred was only twenty-one; he had a secure job and was courting a lovely girl, so suicide seemed unlikely. There was no evidence that anyone had pushed him, so he probably fell in accidentally. The jury returned an open verdict, and the coroner suggested asking the council to put someone formally in charge of the well, and to supply a street light.

The Shoobridges were still grieving for Fred when in 1882 they suffered the excruciating shame of their son Robert's name appearing in the local press because he was arrested for committing an 'unnatural offence' on Christmas Day. He and another lad stood trial for 'laying hands on each other with intent to foster up unnatural desires and to provoke and excite each other to the commission of divers unnatural acts and practices.' The assize judge labelled their conduct 'offensive, disgusting and filthy'. However, because there was only one witness the case was dismissed. Two months later their daughter entered a lunatic asylum,[3] and Mr Shoobridge died the following year. After her son Robert died in 1895, Mrs Shoobridge took her only surviving son to live in a village in Kent, and never set foot in Hastings again.

References: *HSLO* 4 October 1873, 5 November & 24 December 1881; 4 January 1882.

---

2. Described as 'a public house without alcoholic drink...a place where working men may smoke their pipes and sip their coffee and chat away merrily, without one penny being asked of them.'
3. She would spend most of her life in Hellingly, where she eventually died.

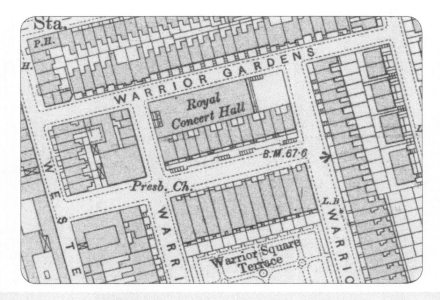

DIGRESSION: THE ROYAL CONCERT HALL

The Concert Rooms, later called the Opera House and Concert Rooms, was renamed the Royal Concert Hall after the Prince and Princess of Wales took lunch there during their visit in 1882. Opened on 13th October 1879. its basement held a large music saloon, with practise and other rooms attached. The ground floor boasted a magnificent concert hall which could accommodate over a thousand people. It measured 97ft by 57ft and had a stage at the east end 55ft wide and 24ft deep. There were performers' dressing-rooms, meeting rooms, reading rooms, card rooms, a capacious billiard-hall accommodating two tables, an indoor tennis court and a shop. It was the first public hall in the borough to be heated. A three-manual pipe organ was custom-built in 1884; some of its thirty-four stops were recycled from the instrument at Lichfield Cathedral, which was then being upgraded.

Many famous performers and musicians played at the RCH, and it was also used for circuses, balls, banquets and political rallies, hosting Winston Churchill MP in 1901, future Prime Minister Mr Asquith MP in 1902 and suffragette leader Mrs Emmeline Pankhurst in 1908. Sadly the main hall was turned into a roller-skating rink, but the other areas continued to host entertainments and functions. It closed in 1918 and stood derelict until 1921, when it reopened as a cinema called the Elite Picture Theatre.

After being bombed in 1940 it was repaired and reopened in 1941, but was soon bombed again. It remained closed until 23rd June 1947. The day it reopened it was completely destroyed by fire. A block of flats called Royal Terrace has occupied the site since 1986.

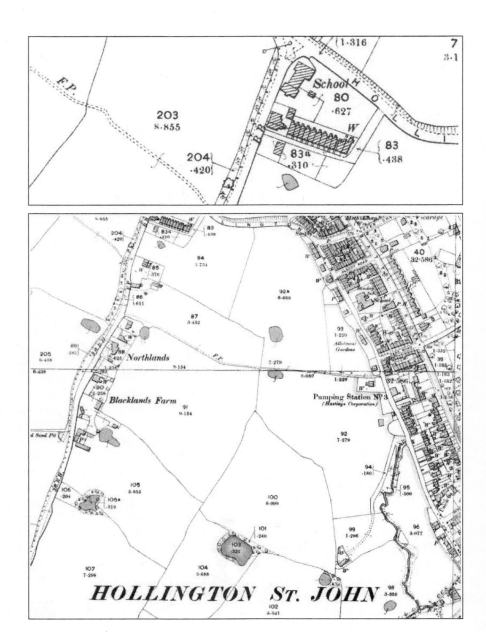

Edward Terrace, close up detail from the larger map.

There were a number of small ponds in the area where William Tompsett and Jesse Oliver lived.

1884

THE IGNORANT RUSTICS

HOLLINGTON

On Wednesday 6th February Coroner Charles Sheppard held an inquest at the Royal Albert Inn, 293 Battle Road, to enquire into the death of Hollington cow-keeper William John Tompsett, aged sixty.

William's wife, brother and son last saw him alive about 6am on Monday, when he walked 'four rods' (20 yards) from his home at 4 Edward Terrace to milk his cow. An hour later his son, Albert, went to the cow lodge but found it locked and his father absent. He broke in, milked the cow, and drove the cans to Hastings to be sold. On the way back he spotted an upturned bucket, with a candle on top, on the bank of a pond. Going closer he saw his father lying in the water, nearly submerged. Having insufficient strength to drag him out, he left to get help.

Meanwhile, the land's owner, Jesse Oliver, saw a group of people standing around his pond, staring at a man lying motionless in the water. Only at his frantic insistence did some men pull him out. Finding him beyond help he remonstrated with them for their lack of compassion towards another human being, but they explained that a policeman must see a dead body before anyone touched it. 'The villagers,' he told the coroner's court, 'kept their belief in the superstition on this occasion to the letter'.

At the inquest the coroner scolded the ignorant Hollington rustics. He 'could not conceive of grosser ignorance' than that which allowed a number of powerful men to stand for nearly an hour round a pond in which a human being lay, without attempting to extricate him. 'For aught anyone might know', he said, 'perhaps the man might have been resuscitated had he been dragged out promptly.' The sooner these yokels 'disabused their minds' of the idea that a body must not be touched until seen by a policeman, the better it would be for 'mankind in general'.

In fact it was more than superstition; police regulations stated that, 'When a dead body is found, and there is no doubt that life is extinct, it should never be touched until the arrival of a constable'. However, it was something of a Catch-22 because the only way to establish that life was indeed extinct was to drag the body out and check for vital signs.

Dr Thomas Harvey gave his opinion that William died from suffocation by drowning, and the jury returned a verdict of suicide.

Reference: *HSLO* 9 February 1884.

86 Albion Street, just prior to demolition in the 1950s.

High Bank is not labelled on this map, but it is in the centre of the image, the long terrace which begins above the words 'Ward By' (boundary). Many of the houses still stand.

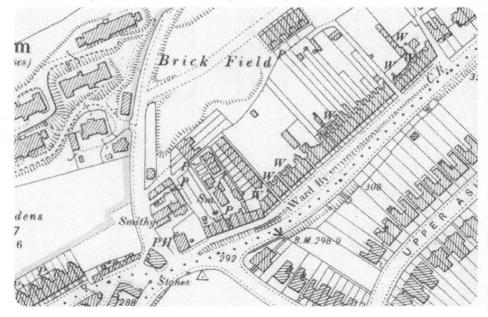

1885

THE WICKED STEPMOTHER

HALTON

The stepmother in the title was baptised Jane Hawes in Salehurst on 29th July 1860. Her parents, Ruth and Robert, were fishmongers in Robertsbridge. The family moved to Lewes, where Ruth died and where, in 1877, Jane, at the age of just sixteen, gave birth to a daughter. The following year they moved to Hastings, where Robert and his brother let wagonettes, hackney carriages and flys, doing the driving themselves.

When the 1881 census was taken, Robert and his second wife were living at 6 Plynlimmon Road with Jane's five-year-old girl, whilst Jane was working as a live-in housemaid at 2 St Margaret's Road. In Hastings Workhouse on 29th October 1881 she gave birth to her second child, Alfred. When he was two she became pregnant again. The father of her third child was William Carr, a recently-widowed gasworks employee.

Carr was born on 12th March 1853, the son of a carpenter. His family also moved to Hastings when he was a teenager, and rented 61 St Mary's Terrace. He married and had three sons, but two died in infancy. The 1881 census shows him and his wife lodging at 20 Manor Road with their only surviving child, Alfred, who was then three months old, having been born on 9th February. When William registered the birth he signed with an X, revealing the extent of his illiteracy: he was unable to write even his own name. His wife died in July 1882 and eight months later he made Jane Hawes pregnant.

Jane and William wed in July 1883, when she was twenty-three and he thirty. Each brought to the marriage a toddler called Alfred. Although Jane's son was eight months younger than William's, he was bigger, and so was nicknamed 'Jumbo'. Four months after their wedding a daughter, Celia Jane, was born.

William had been employed by the gasworks for fifteen years and earned 5s a day as a stoker. He worked seven days a week, alternating weeks of nights and day shifts. Jane's job was to look after the two boys and the new baby.

Between November 1883 and August 1884 the Carrs lodged with the King family at 32 Whitefriars Road. They had two rooms: a kitchen-cum-living room and a bedroom, in which Celia was born soon after they moved in. Mrs King saw William's son Alfred shrink from a plump, healthy boy to a thin, sick-looking one. He would sometimes beg her for food, which she gave him in secret. She was not the only neighbour who noticed this ill treatment. About 20th May Martha Starr at no.33 visited Relieving Officer Edward Apps to report her concerns. The following month Apps visited with a colleague, Alfred Hastings, to find little

Alfred tucking heartily into a raisin pudding whilst sporting a black eye. They took no action except to send Dr Ashenden, who told Jane Carr not to beat Alfred but to give him 'sea-water baths, and puddings'.

Jane was aware that she was being monitored, and that she was known to the authorities, yet she did not change her childrearing technique. When the Carrs moved out in August, Mrs King called into the police station in Hastings Town Hall because she was worried sick about Alfred. The police ignored her.

From August to November the Carrs rented a small house in Albion Street, Halton.[1] Their next door neighbour at no.3, teenager Jessie Lawrence, earned cash helping Jane Carr with the household chores. She told her mother that Alfred was being mistreated, and her mother reported it to the police. This time, D.S. James Love visited Jane Carr at the end of August. She admitted: 'I have beat him, but not more than I consider necessary to try to correct him of his dirty habits'. Clearly he was not potty-trained. In response to yet another complaint James Love returned a fortnight later, but the boy seemed fine to him. Jane was angry and demanded to know who had accused her.

Mrs Rummery, who lived at no.87, had raised seven children of her own, and could see that Alfred was being neglected. She asked Dr Hammond to call round, and they visited the Carrs together. Jane said that Alfred was given plenty of food, but suffered from 'consumption of the bowels' and she could not afford a doctor. Hammond advised her to obtain a ticket for the infirmary, then she could get free treatment. He issued a stern warning that if Alfred were to die 'in that state under her care, she would be tried for manslaughter and severely punished'.

Carr, furious at Mrs Rummery for 'meddling' in his private business, stormed to her house and issued a string of threats peppered with expletives. If she interfered again, he promised to kick her out and 'do for' her. She suggested offering the boy for adoption to someone who wanted a child. Carr refused, saying that 'the little beast deserves all he gets; he is always stealing food'.

In November the Carrs moved to 4 Alma Cottages, on the High Bank on Old London Road, where a four-roomed house 'with copper, kitchener and pump' cost 4s a week. On 12th December the parish doctor, Walter Jones, a young man with a child the same age as Alfred, called round to examine him. Jones thought he had a 'pallid look' which suggested a wasting disease, but gave no medicine and suggested no treatment.

On 12th January Jane Carr asked Mrs Lawrence to come in and take a look at Alfred. He was insensible and, the neighbour suspected, 'in a dying state'. However, Jane refused to call a doctor. Mrs Lawrence went immediately to Dr Jones, who left it until the following day to call upon Jane. As he stood on the doorstep she pointed to a lively boy, brimming with good health, running about in the front parlour behind her, and asked the doctor, 'There does not seem much the matter with him now, does there?' Jane had deliberately misled Dr Jones: the boy he saw was her own well nourished son, 'Jumbo'.

1. Albion Street and those surrounding were demolished in the 1950s. Halton flats occupy the site.

Mrs Lawrence returned yet again to the police, and this time she was so insistent that the superintendent himself decided to pay a surprise visit to the Carrs. He would take Dr Jones with him, and they would turn up at 1am. When they arrived the doctor went upstairs and saw a little boy he had never laid eyes on before. It was a bitterly cold winter's night, and the poor mite lay in his iron crib barely covered by a thin and filthy blanket. He was shockingly emaciated and his scanty clothing was 'wet through from urine'. His feet were 'in a frightful congested condition' from the cold, and one of his big toes was 'almost gangrenous from want of attention'. The men left and the next day the superintendent discussed the case with the relieving officer.

On Thursday 22nd January Dr Jones was called to examine William Carr, who was lying in bed with rheumatism, but whilst there he took another look at Alfred. He was much the same. The next morning Jane woke at 8am to find Alfred cold and dead in his iron crib. She walked to Dr Jones's house and informed him. That night, in the front bedroom at Alma Cottages, and accompanied by a police constable, he conducted the post mortem. A healthy weight for a four-year-old was about 40lb, but Alfred weighed only 25lb. 'There was hardly an atom of fat' on him, Jones recorded.

The inquest was opened at the Hare and Hounds Inn (opposite Christ Church on Old London Road) the next evening, by Coroner Charles Sheppard. The jury was taken to view the body, and depositions were given by Dr Jones and the Carrs. William emphasised that Alfred had been a delicate boy and therefore susceptible to ill health. He denied any abuse. Jane described her stepson as 'dull and shrivelled' and claimed that, whilst she dealt him the odd slap for soiling himself, she never beat him. The inquest was adjourned. When it resumed on Tuesday 27th January the shocking accounts of cruelty related by former neighbours Jane and Alice King, Caroline Rummery and Jessie Lawrence led the jury to return a verdict of manslaughter. The coroner committed the Carrs to stand trial at the Sussex Assizes in Lewes in February.

After a night locked in Hastings Gaol, the Carrs were brought before two county magistrates, ex-Indian Army Colonel Henry Lane of Broadoak Manor in Bexhill and wealthy landowner Horatio Marriott. The police charged the Carrs with wilful murder. After hearing from Dr Jones, Mrs King and Jessie Lawrence, the magistrates concurred and remanded them until the following Saturday.

The magistrates' court was inside the town hall; however, the police were acutely aware of the strength of local feeling against people who abused children and expected a mob to gather outside. To outwit them, the hearing was conducted at 44a Robertson Street, the office of the Clerk to the Justices, solicitor F.A. Langham.[2] The building had a rear exit into an alley which led to Claremont Steps. Angry locals discovered the ruse and an ever-growing mob assembled outside in order to 'wreak their vengeance upon the prisoners'. One canny protester realised that by standing on the corner of Claremont they could keep both exits in sight and pounce on the Carrs the instant they emerged.

2. Frederick Adolphus, son of James George Langham, known as 'the smugglers' solicitor'.

Robertson Street in 1875. The building far left, named Trinity House, is no.44, which had Mr Blomfield's photographic studio on the ground floor and Mr Langham's office above.

When a cab drew up in Robertson Street, half-a-dozen constables surrounded the Carrs to protect them as they walked to the vehicle. Despite this a handful of the mob rushed forward and the couple 'narrowly escaped being lynched'. A policeman's helmet was sent flying as officers tried to hold back the enraged locals. One woman almost managed to strike Mrs Carr; another suddenly lunged forward and spat right in her face. The cab drove 'at a rapid pace' to Warrior Square station and the Carrs were escorted on the 4.20 train to Lewes, where they were held in prison for three weeks whilst awaiting trial.

The first edition of the *HSLO* to cover the story was that of 31st January. Under the headline 'Alleged Case of Starvation', readers learned that 'Intense interest has been excited' by the inquest, which revealed 'a long course of systematic ill-treatment'. The editor wrote that 'the heart is moved to loathing for the man and woman Carr, and to deep sorrow for the poor little four-year-old.' It 'thrills one with horror', he added, 'to think that anyone in Hastings could treat a child so...Few can read the report without being moved to indignation', he concluded, 'many will be unable to overcome their feelings sufficiently' to read to the end'. On the same day these words were published, Alfred was interred at the Borough Cemetery, 'the relatives of the father carrying everything out in a suitable manner'.

During the eighteen months between the Carr's marriage and Alfred's death, they both had relations living nearby. Jane's father was well known all over town for taking parties around the countryside in his horse-drawn wagonette, and as a successful fly proprietor who lived for decades in a prominent double-fronted villa, 30 Devonshire Road. He married again and had a son in 1884. William's parents and three of his siblings resided at 17 All Saints' Street, next to the Stag Inn. His brother, who lived in Bourne Walk, also had a child in 1884. Unless the couple was estranged from them, surely their relatives visited and wanted their children to meet their uncles, aunts and cousins. Yet there is no mention of these relations in any press report.

The details of the cruelty meted out to Alfred was divulged by the Carrs' female neighbours from the witness stands of three courts. The following account omits the most unsavoury details but, for the sake of historical record, their testimonies are reproduced on pages 102–3.

The trial

The Carrs were tried at Sussex Assizes in Lewes over two days, 13th and 14th February. Known as 'the Ore Manslaughter Case', it was discussed at kitchen tables and in parlours and beershops throughout Hastings, and there was much speculation about what sentences the accused were likely to get.

When it emerged that Jane Carr had lived in Lewes as a child this increased local interest. Each time the couple were transferred between Lewes Gaol and the court in a horse-drawn prison van (complete with police escort), swarms of angry people gathered, eager to make their feelings known. The Carrs were hissed and booed and the van was chased along the streets by 'mobs of boys, hooting and howling'.

In the dock the Carrs, who were described as being 'of imperfect education', looked 'dejected and haggard' as they were charged with 'killing and slaying Alfred Carr', and with unlawfully neglecting to provide with 'proper care and attention, food and other necessaries, whereby his health was endangered, and his life placed in great peril'. They pleaded not guilty.

Lord Coleridge, the Lord Chief Justice of England, began by reducing the indictment from murder to manslaughter. The prosecution was conducted by H.C. Richards and E.M. Hall; the defence counsel comprised C.F. Gill and T.E. Cundy. Mr Richards said it was his 'very painful duty' to have to speak about the 'harrowing' details. The systematic ill-treatment was known of solely because of the Carr's neighbours, who were 'impelled by that genuine feeling of womanhood to protest against the ill-treatment of a poor little struggling, puny, tiny child.' Upon his death, Mr Richards continued, when Alfred died, he was 'at last released...from an earthly father here, where it had nothing but ill-treatment, to another Father, who would receive it in a very different manner'.

DIGRESSION: THE LEGAL TEAM

Henry Charles Richards, later a KC and an MP, was the son of Frederick, a JP at Ore and St Leonards, where he lived at Caerhage, West Hill Road. H.C. paid for a cross to be erected in Hastings to commemorate the coronation of Edward VII. Hall and Gill were bright young barristers who would later become Sir Charles Frederick Gill KC, Director of Public Prosecutions, and Sir Edward Marshall Hall KC. Hall lived at 30 Old Steine, Brighton, was the most celebrated legal figure of his era. Known as 'The Great Defender', several books have been written about his life, and in 1996 the BBC presented a radio series, presented by John Mortimer, in which six of his trials were dramatised.

Sir Charles Frederick Gill KC
A chromolithograph by Sir Leslie Ward published in *Vanity Fair* on 9th May 1891

Defence counsel Mr Gill, who addressed the jury for two hours, was 'thoroughly alive' to his difficult position, because nothing was harder to defend than the ill treatment of a child. He was reduced to the barrel-scraping suggestion that one neighbour, Mrs King, had 'grossly exaggerated everything' and 'magnified gossip'. Denying accusations that his clients were guilty of 'culpable negligence' or 'wanton brutality', he argued that the boy died not from ill treatment but because he was 'delicate and scrofulous'. Mrs Carr left him naked sometimes simply because he repeatedly 'dirtied himself' and, through poverty, she had insufficient changes of clothing for him.

Unusually, the jury did not need to retire to a private room to discuss and agree upon a verdict: they found the accused guilty as charged. William and Jane then stood in the dock and waited to be addressed directly by the judge, Lord Coleridge, who told them:

> You have been found guilty of cruel, wicked, detestable conduct to an unoffending child; unoffending, I say, because its habits were hardly under its control, and if they had been, then you went the way to make it worse. Both of you forgot the commonest principles of moralists of your duty towards the child.

Because William was at work while most of the abuse took place, the judge sentenced him to 18 months' with hard labour, then turned his attention to Jane: 'I must mark my sense of what I consider your cruel, unwomanly and cowardly conduct, I order you into penal servitude for ten years.' Jane exclaimed, 'Oh, my God! What a long time!' and was removed from the dock crying bitterly. She was conducted down to the cells sobbing and wailing, 'My poor child; my baby!' She was referring to little Celia, not the stepson she had killed.

According to the *HSLO* the sentence 'felt like a thunderbolt...upon the miserable woman', who had 'buoyed herself up' with the hope that, if she did not escape, her punishment would not be a heavy one. Her shrieks, and her despairing cry of, 'Lord have mercy upon me', when she learned...that her life for the next ten years must be passed as a convict among convicts, and amid all the horrors of penal servitude, showed how little she had realised the terrible gravity of her position.' The writer added: 'few of us in Hastings could have imagined...such a long sentence'. The general concensus had been that she would get between two and seven years. However, he approved of the penalty and remarked:

> The woman having stepped into the shoes of the natural protector of the child, was bound by every precept of God and man to behave as a mother to the poor little innocent, but instead she abused this trust reposed in her — abused it grossly, wickedly, cruelly, and most cowardly. We may well hope that Jane Carr is an abnormal type of a step-mother, and that Hastings will never again know another of her species.

He regretted that Carr, 'that black-hearted, mean, cowardly fellow' received such a short sentence: 'To my mind, Carr was worse than his she-demon of a wife.'

The following week the *HSLO* mentioned 'a rumour afloat in this borough that Jane Carr...had died in Lewes Gaol.' If true', opined the editor, 'we can only say, "Let her deeds perish with her".' In fact she had severe 'inflammation of the bowels', and her father had visited her, setting the gossips' tongues wagging.

The story was widely reported across the UK, Canada and Australia. One newsman described it as 'a revolting case of domestic cruelty...The wanton savagery...makes one of the most sickening stories ever read.' Jane had decided that the boy 'must be got rid of' and acted 'with a deliberate barbarity that would have revolted a primitive savage'. Alfred's delicate disposition 'seems only to have whetted the mother's hatred'. He believed that Mrs Carr should 'have been sent to prison for the term of her natural life'. William was also 'too lightly punished', and Mr Apps ought to be sacked. In fact, all the officials and authorities involved failed to take action quickly enough and would have Alfred's death on their conscience evermore.

Jane was not sent to Lewes Gaol but to Woking Female Penitentiary in Surrey, where ill prisoners were housed. Where William Carr served his time at an unknown location. His year and place of death be established.

Jane Carr did not serve her ten-year sentence. On 5th June 1886 she died of tubercular meningitis in the prison infirmary, at the age of just twenty-five. Her body was brought back to Hastings, where she was buried in the Borough Cemetery.

Jane's daughter Ruth was raised by her grandparents. She became a live-in kitchenmaid at a large boarding house at 28 Cornwallis Gardens, hiding her parentage by giving a false surname. After marrying in 1897 she moved to London, had twelve children and died of cancer at the age of forty-four.

When her parents were imprisoned, legal responsibility for the care of fifteen-month-old Celia Carr devolved to the Hastings Union. She was baptised and boarded out (fostered), to a coachman's family in Kent. As an adult she moved to London where, in 1906, she had a child and subsequently made a good marriage with a legal clerk who went on to have a highly respectable career as a civil servant. They produced five children and lived a conventional middle-class life in a villa in south London. She died in 1939 at the age of fifty-six.

Alfred 'Jumbo' Hawes was taken into Hastings Workhouse. In 1897 he enlisted in the Coldstream Guards, in which he served for eleven years. When he married in 1906 he lied about his paternity, telling the registrar his father was 'Alfred Hawes, jeweller'. He and his wife emigrated to Toronto, and had four daughters. He became a sergeant major in the Royal Grenadiers, and during the First World War, served in France and was decorated for bravery and for being 'zealous' about his men's wellbeing. After an action-packed life he died in Canada at the age of forty-seven.

| Ninth January 1881. Manor Road, S¹ Mary in the Castle U S D | Alfred Ernest | Boy | William Carr | Celia Carr formerly Golding | Stoker Gasworks | The mark of William Carr Father Manor Road Hastings |

When and Where Died.	Name and Surname.	Sex.	Age.	Rank or Profession.	Cause of Death.
Twenty third January 1885, 4 Alma Cottages Ore R S D	Alfred Carr	Male	4 years	Child of William Carr a Stoker at the Hastings Gasworks	Systematic illtreatment and Starvation manslaughter against William Carr and Jane Carr

Details from Alfred Ernest Carr's birth and death certificates. The first reveals that William Carrr was illiterate and was only about to make an X instead of signing. William's mother was Celia Carr, née Golding. The death certificate gives the cause as 'Systematic illtreatment and starvation. Manslaughter against Willian Carr and Jane Carr'.

References: *HSLO* 31 January and 7, 14 and 21 February 1885; *Witney Gazette* 21 February 1885; *Mid Sussex Times* and *Horsham Express* 17 February 1885; *Evening Standard* 2 February 1885; *The People* 1 February 1885.

Artist's impression sketch of William and Jane Carr and Alfred, from *The Illustrated Police News*.

Evidence given by witnesses Jane King and her daugher, Alice, and of Louisa Bolingbroke, relating to the cruelty of Jane Carr towards her stepson Alfred.

Jane King: Jane Carr was very unkind and cruel to Alfred. I have seen her bang him on the floor and beat him with a stick. It was a large, thick walking stick, or the handle of an umbrella. I remonstrated with her, and begged of her to be kind and be a mother to him. She replied, 'The little beast, he deserves it; he is dirty.' I never saw him without bruises or marks of some kind. I have seen them on his face, legs and body. I have known him shut in the closet when they had meals. The child had often begged food of me, and I have given it him in his mother's absence, but not when she was present, or she would beat him. The father was kind to the child at first, but later he was cruel. The child was dirty in its habits night and day; I did not think he could help himself. I think being punished might have caused him to be in that state.

Alice King: I am 13. I have seen Mrs. Carr hold his hands and beat him with a stick till the fingernails were blue and bleeding, and the hand puffed up. I have seen her lay him across her lap and beat him with Mr. Carr's low shoe. Sometimes she beat him with a hearth brush, and sometimes with a stick. She sometimes beat him for nothing. Sometimes he was dressed, sometimes he wasn't. He asked for food, and I used to give it to him if his mother had gone out. The child was easily frightened. I have seen his little head in a filthy condition with vermin. If he did not obey Jane Carr, she used to beat him. I used to tell my mother about it. The boy used to have his food more regular when the father was home, if he had been a good boy. If he was naughty, he used to have to go without.

Mrs Carr used to say he kept food in the roof of his mouth, and she used to have a stick and poke it round his mouth, and then push it down his throat. I saw that done twice. She said he did not swallow it. I have seen Mrs. Carr shove hard crusts of bread down his throat. I have seen her pull him along by the hair of his head. I have seen him shut up in a closet. That was sometimes when Mrs. Carr went out, and sometimes when he was dirty. The boy seemed frightened to ask his mother to let him go to the closet, but he had asked me when we were alone. I have had seen him washed and whipped afterwards. During the time he was with them he seemed to get worse. He had sores and bruises on different parts of his body.

Louisa Bolingbroke: I am 15. I would mind the children while Jane Carr was out, and take them out as well. Mrs. Carr used to beat Alfred with her hand, and with a stick sometimes. I have also seen her take hold of the hair of his head and drag him along. He was always beaten when he was dirty, and sometimes when he was not. Alfred often asked me for food and when she was out. I used to take him to Mrs. King; she fed him. I showed her the bruises on his body. I have seen him locked up in a cupboard for four or five hours. I have only seen the father correct him when he had made a mess in the room. The child's dirty habits continued. He never got better of it. He was very pale and delicate. He was not like other children. It used to stand still and did not dare move. Jumbo and the baby used to go out nearly every day, but Alfred did not. I only took him out about six times during the time she was there.

Evidence given by witnesses Caroline Rummery, Elizabeth Lawrence and doctors Edward Hammond and Walter Grant Jones.

Caroline Rummery: I once saw Jane Carr with a brush in her hand and a pail by her side, and the little boy quite naked standing in the wash-house. I saw blood running down his left leg. Blood was also flowing from the left arm. He had a very bad black eye, and there was some sticking plaster on his head. I said, 'Mrs, Carr, take him in the kitchen, poor little dear, he looks dying.' She replied, 'The little beast, I hate him.' I went to fetch Dr. Hammond and I took him to the Carrs' house. I asked where the child was, and it was in the corner of the room behind a chair.

Elizabeth Lawrence: I saw the child first when they were living at High Bank. The child looked as if it was recovering from illness. I spoke to the child, and it was very intelligent. It was frightened, but it had a pretty way of speaking, and was well behaved. You never gave the child a thing, but what he would say, 'Thank you, lady,' 'Please lady.' I went into the house once when Mrs. Carr was out and gave the child some bread and treacle. On 12th January Mrs Carr asked me to look at Alfred. I went in, and saw him in a cradle in an insensible condition. He threw his head about. I thought he was in a dying state, and told her so. I also told her to send for a doctor. She said, 'Dying? He's not dying, he has been like this before in the Whitefriars-road.' I told her to send for a doctor, or she would get herself into trouble. Three hours afterwards I went back and he was standing in the room trembling as if he could hardly stand, and was eating a very large piece of bread ravenously. I said, 'Why did you not let him lie down, or sit before the fire?' The female prisoner replied that she wanted him to get the use of his legs. I saw him no more.

Dr Edward E. Hammond: I saw the boy at Mrs. Rummery's request. It had bruises on its arms and legs, and looked very ill, very pale, and emaciated. A child in good health would take some weeks to be in an emaciated condition. I asked Mrs Carr how it was the child was in that state, and whether she had supplied it with sufficient nourishment. Her answer was: 'Yes, the child has always had plenty of food.'

Dr Walter Grant Jones: I visited the house with the Superintendent of Police on the Friday before the child died. I saw a child I had not previously seen, in an iron crib. There was either a rug or a blanket in a filthy state covering it. It had a small shirt on, and seemed terribly frightened. I said the child wanted to be kept warm, properly attended to, and properly fed.

I made a post mortem. I found the body in very emaciated state. There was a cut in the forehead about half an inch long, above the right eye. There was no fat on the body, inside or out. There were sores behind each knee, both feet were immensely congested, and were of a dark purple colour. The big toe on the right foot was commencing to be gangrenous. All the internal organs were healthy. I found no trace of any disease. The brain was healthy. The stomach was very much distended with gas, but contained a small quantity of food. The small intestines were also distended. In my opinion the cause of the child's death was the want of proper care and proper and sufficient food.

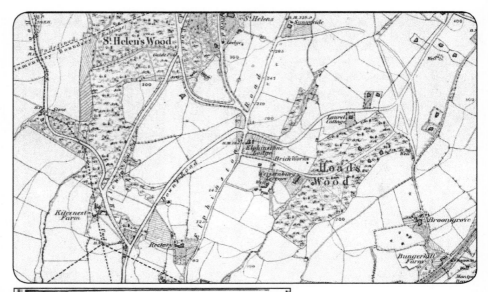

Map of the area in 1873.

Advert from 1879.

Jesmond Dene today.

Strong Poison

Blacklands

Until the 1870s the area now called Blacklands was part of the Blacklands Estate, comprising farmland with a few buildings, bounded by Kite's Nest Farm, Ore Valley Fields and St Helen's Park woods. The owner, Mr Frewen[1], bought the land in 1861 from Maria Sayer. He was not local but in 1856 he married widow Frances Brisco of nearby Coghurst Hall. After she died in 1867 Frewen commissioned a church to be built in her memory (Christ Church) and sold the land around it in plots to property developers. On it they built over 100 substantial, elegant, spacious villas, marketing the area as 'the most pleasant and healthy spot in Hastings'.

These houses provided not only luxurious new homes for middle class families but also gainful employment for hundreds of young women as housemaids, cooks, parlourmaids and nursery maids. Adverts variously demanded that prospective servants be respectable, sober, church-going and trustworthy, and some specified a preference for country-bred girls.

Alice Foster, twenty-two, and her sister Minnie, sixteen, were among the highly sought-after country girls, having grown up at New Cut, Westfield. Their father was a humble farm labourer; their mother was perpetually pregnant, giving birth to eleven children. The girls were lucky to find jobs working together, which would stave off loneliness and home-sickness. They became the only residential servants employed at Jesmond Dene, a new villa in Baldslow Road. Their job was to help a young mother, Mary Banks, to run the house and look after a four-year-old girl, Edith, and a baby boy.

Mary's father, William Andrews, was the highly esteemed Borough Surveyor of Hastings. She married Charles Banks at St Andrew's church in 1883. He was a corn merchant, fly proprietor and Sunday School teacher.

After work on Wednesday 13th May 1891 Charles walked the few steps from his office at 11 Queen's Road to the Floral Hall at no.13 (now Gregg's) to buy weed killer from Mrs Gilbert. She stocked it in gallon cans so, needing only an eighth of that amount, he took along an empty bottle made of black glass and bearing a label showing its former contents: 'Scotch Elder Wine'. Shop assistant

---

1. Charles Hay Frewen was MP for East Sussex 1846–1857. His elder brother Thomas inherited Brickwall House, Northiam. His younger brother Moreton married an aunt of Winston Churchill and lived at Brede Place. Moreton's daughter, sculptor Clare Sheridan, was the best frlived in Hastings Old Town. She was best friends with Ghita Stanhope (see 'Bedstead and Bootlace').

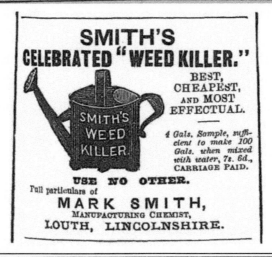
Whilst only George Gilbert's name appeared on adverts, his wife Harriet managed the Queen's Road shop whilst he worked in their market-garden at Harold Road, producing many of the items sold in the shop. The business was taken over by the Hussey family in the 1940s. The Floral Hall was no.13 Queens' Road, which is now Gregg's. The building that housed Charles's office, no.11, was demolished to widen Albert Road.

Advert in the *HSLO* in 1889, possibly the one Alice Foster replied to, bringing her sister in later as nursemaid to the children. In 1891 more than a million girls and women were 'in service' in the UK and servants' registry offices and classified ads matched employers with workers.

Advert from the *Agricultural Journal* of 2nd May 1891, just a few days before the accident.

Ernest Barton decanted a pint of Smith's Weed Killer into the bottle. It was to be diluted four parts to 100 parts of water, so a pint would last for years. That evening Charles pasted on a home made label bearing the words 'Weed killer' and left the bottle at the far end of the garden with the new label facing forwards.

After dinner Charles and Mary went out. Little Edith played in the garden, found the bottle and carried it indoors, placing it on the scullery table. About 9.15pm Minnie spotted a bottle, labelled as elderberry wine. It had been opened and some was missing, so she tried some, just to see what it tasted like. Discovering it was utterly vile she spat it out into the sink. Alice came in and, wondering what made Minnie do that, examined the bottle. She drew her sister's attention to the 'weed killer' label. Minnie had not seen it, as the bottle had been turned the other way. Alice was deeply concerned, but Minnie assured her she had not swallowed much, if any. However, after a while she started to feel ill.

When their employers arrived home they were informed of the situation. Charles hurried to 85 Mount Pleasant Road to fetch surgeon Mr Adkins. He found Minnie lying on a couch clutching her stomach in pain and vomiting into a bowl. The doctor administered some medicine and promised to return later. Alice and Mary sat with her into the early hours. She seemed to get worse, and at 2.40am Charles went again to fetch Mr Adkins. By the time they arrived at Minnie's bedside, she was dead.

The inquest was held at the Langham Hotel by Mr W.J. Glenister, in the presence of the chief constable. Mr Adkins explained that his post mortem found internal inflammation consistent with arsenical poisoning. His analysis of the weed killer showed it contained arsenic, caustic soda and methylated spirit.

The coroner placed no blame on Mr Banks, nor on Minnie. The shop was wholly at fault. He asked Mr Barton why he had not warned Mr Banks that weed killer was a poison; the young man replied that he thought that was obvious to everyone. The coroner pointed out that, under the Sale of Poisons Act, only a chemist could sell arsenic. He was therefore duty bound to report the matter (and send the bottle) to the Pharmaceutical Society and leave its officials to decide whether action would be taken against Mrs Gilbert. The jury returned a verdict of 'death through misadventure'.

After Minnie Foster died, Charles and Mary Banks moved from 50 to 40 Baldslow Road, where they lived for nearly forty years. During the 1890s they added one more child to the family and Mary's parents moved in with them.

References: HSLO 28 April & 23 June 1888; 16 May 1891; 22 February 1896; 27 August 1921. The Chemist and Druggist 23 May 1891.

DIGRESSION: WILLIAM ANDREWS

Mr Andrews was Borough Surveyor from 1861 until 1888, a period when Hastings transformed from a small town into a large, populous one. He arrived here in his early thirties and ended up being 'one of the grand old men' of the town, which he would traverse in a pony phaeton.

He designed, developed or managed many important improvements, but his greatest achievements were the town's water supply and drainage system and the building of the Parade and sea walls to protect the foreshore. In 1870 he designed the new sewage system and when a terrible tragedy happened late one night he rushed to the scene to help (see 'Three Men Down' in Volume One). He also supervised the laying out of several pleasure grounds, including Alexandra Park.

William Andrews was undoubtedly a workaholic. During extensive projects he would work round the clock, 'sometimes without seeing his bed for several nights'. His time with the council had been twenty-seven years of 'arduous toil and constant anxiety'. One alderman regretted that, by over-conscientious attention to duty Mr Andrews had 'ruined his health'. Hastings, it was said, 'depended more upon the ability of the Surveyor than upon anyone else'. In Mr Andrews's hands, the town 'had been kept in capital order' and it 'would never meet with a more faithful or competent servant'.

In 1888 Mr Andrews was obliged to resign due to ill health. His workmen organised a collection and bought him a 'handsome and massive' marble and bronze clock with Gothic pillars, and a costly, silver-mounted ebony walking-stick. At his leaving party, their spokesman called him 'the most upright and honest of masters'. The corporation gave him a banquet and an illuminated address, and its members praised him most generously for his great contribution to the town's position as 'the premier watering-place'. He was an 'honest, attentive, obliging and courteous' man of 'insight and integrity', who was 'beloved by all who knew him' and, what was more, 'his smiling face and genial manner won the hearts of all with whom he came into contact.'

Mr Andrews's salary was £375 a year, and the corporation offered him a yearly stipend of £200 to stay on as 'consulting surveyor' to his replacement, Mr Palmer, whose salary was to be £400. One councillor argued that the new surveyor should only get £300, especially as he had the help of Mr Andrews. Ratepayers were now going to pay £600 instead of £375, for no good reason. Another asserted that starting a man on £400 gave him 'no inducement to improve himself'.

In the 1890s Andrews and his wife moved in with their daughter and son-in-law at 40 Baldslow Road, where both spent the rest of their lives; indeed, Andrews died in the house in 1902. The editor of the *HSLO* mentioned that he had been paid his stipend until his death.

SHAFTED

QUEEN'S ROAD BRIDGE

Nowadays Queen's Road extends from the Halifax to the roundabout next to Alexandra Park. The road existed by the 1840s, but until 1876 the south section (as far as Bedford Place, where Santander is now) was called Meadow Road and until 1887 the north section was known as St Andrew's Road. That name derived from an ancient church that once stood on the west side of the Castle hill, until it was plundered by the French and fell into ruin.

When the railway was being built between Hastings and Rye in 1849, the line had to cross high above the north end of St Andrew's Road, so an embankment was built to support it. To let the road through, a 120ft tunnel was dug through the embankment and lined with six courses of bricks. Internally it was 16ft high and 21ft wide, of which three feet on each side was pavement. A gas lamp was placed about half way through, but it did little to illuminate the gloomy interior.

At the time this shadowy tube of bricks, named St Andrew's Archway, lay on the outskirts of town, and its width and height, though diminutive, were perfectly adequate because there were only a few houses and farms dotted about to the north of it, and the modest traffic consisted of pedestrians, equestrians, carts and carriages. In 1864 a park, also named for St Andrew, was opened close to the north portal.

The name of St Andrew was again chosen when a residential square was laid out just south of the gasworks and yet again when a new church was built. It was opened on (predictably) St Andrew's Day in 1870 and soon children in the new parish were attending the associated St Andrew's Schools.[1]

The 1870s saw exponential residential growth on the north side of the railway line. Dozens of new roads and hundreds of new homes were built, spreading across St Helen's and Blacklands, and snaking around both sides of the park, which was gradually being enlarged and laid out more formally and with more amenities. There was an associated huge increase in road traffic, and horse-drawn omnibuses also began to use the archway, which was becoming unfit for purpose. In 1877 an alderman flagged up the need to improve the structure; it was less than thirty years old and yet was already being referred to as a 'rat hole'.

1. St. Andrew's Church survived 100 years. The site is now covered by Morrisons petrol station, whilst the parish of St Andrew was united with that of Christ Church, Blacklands.

The north portal looking from Ore Lane (now Mount Pleasant Road) shortly after the railway line was built on the embankment seen in the centre of this painting. The line of white buildings is St Andrew's Road. The tall black chimneys are at the gas works, now the site of Morrisons. The area around the north end of the tunnel was then rural, but is now the site of a roundabout junction of five roads and the entrance to Alexandra Park.

The south portal in 1896.

In April 1882 a survey was undertaken. From 5.30am to 9pm, 8,312 foot passengers and 1,615 vehicles and horses passed through the archway. At the busiest time, noon till 2 pm, the numbers using it reached 1,000 an hour.

The archway lay on the route from the town centre to Blacklands. To get to school, many children walked along its narrow pavements, often in groups, whilst horses, carts and carriages passed by, perilously close. With only fifteen feet of road-width aavailable, when two horse-drawn vehicles passed each other not only was the width filled but horses, unlike cars, did not keep in a straight line, nor were they neatly streamlined but had various bits of paraphernalia sticking out and rattling about. Sometimes, to be safe, those on the pavement had to stand with their their backs against the wall as vehicles passed.

In 1886 a Sussex newspaper remarked that, 'The traffic through the arch is immense and it is a marvel there are not more accidents'. Near-misses were a daily occurrence, and there were frequent accidents, sometimes involving children.The council blamed drivers' excessive speed, and from 1887 printed boards were exhibited at both ends, bearing the words: 'CAUTION. In order to obviate risk of accident, it is requested that all drivers of vehicles and riders will proceed at a walking pace through this Archway. By Order, GEORGE MEADOWS, Town Clerk. The mishaps, however, continued, because there were too many words to read from a moving vehicle. Within a few years they were replaced by signs bearing the curt and emphatic order: 'DRIVE SLOWLY'.

Food delivery vehicles serving the new houses were the biggest menace because the drivers, usually youths, made the trips so often that they became bored slow-trotting along the same routes, and began speeding to inject a bit of excitement into their humdrum working day. One local complained that the 'impudent butchers driving at their usual break-neck pace down the slope of Elphinstone Road, turn the corner sharply and dash through the Archway... caring nothing whom they may run over.' In 1892 'Onlooker' remarked:

> I quite expect one of these days that someone will be killed...Only a short time ago a trap was overturned at its entrance. I myself was once an eyewitness of a horse and cart running away through it. No one has yet been killed in the Archway; therefore I have come to the conclusion that the Council are waiting until that takes place.

From the early 1880s the privately-mumbled derogatory comments and epithets began to be aired publicly. Prominent local William Ransom observed in 1882 that the 'dungeon-like' archway 'casts a gloom over one of the prettiest spots'. According to one town councillor, using it was 'more like going through a sewer than a road', whilst another local man revealed: 'You have to put a pocket handkerchief to your mouth in passing through it'.

By the mid-1880s nobody was able to refer to the archway without tagging on a disparaging adjective. Here are some random descriptions gleaned from the *HSLO* between 1885 and 1896:

'A dreary cavern.'
'A horrible man trap.'
'A huge abomination.'
'Hideous, miserable, disgraceful.'
'Unhealthy, dangerous and unsightly.'
'The ugly memorial of bricks and mortar.'
That monument of the apathy of our ruling powers.'
'A positive danger to the lives of those passing through it.'
'Unsanitary and unsavoury...vile, dirty and ill-smelling.'
'A source of danger and a standing menace.'
'A foul, ill-smelling, enlarged rat-hole.'
'A hideous, foul-smelling death-trap.'
'A dangerous obstruction.'
'A wretched structure.'
'Disgusting.'

It was even called a 'foul, noisome structure' by an estate agent in an advert offering a nearby property (143 Queen's Road) for sale!

In the *HSLO* in 1887, 'Vox Populi' pulled no punches. The archway, he asserted, was 'a hideous railway abortion...Its excessive length, narrow span, low, maimed arch, rumbling reverberations and oppressive gloom might suggest a route to Hades, but for glimpses of real life, and occasional collisions between omnibuses and milk-carts'.

Nobody had greater opportunity to air his views than the editor of the *HSLO*. Between 1882 and 1896 he called it 'the St Andrew's Road Eyesore'; 'a vile thing, at times as offensive to the smell as it is disagreeable to the eye'; 'scarcely fit for a lady to pass through'; a 'dismal hole'; 'the absolute trap to life and limb'; 'a dark, foul opening' which 'disfigured and defiled' the approach to the park; and a 'dirty, repulsive brick structure' which was a 'foul blot on the fair face of the town' and a 'drawback to its good name.' It ought to be 'razed to the ground as speedily as possible.' In 1895 he grumbled that it 'continues to rear its foul and ugly head' and looked forward to the day when the 'abominable erection has been swept away'. 'Many speeches have been made in denunciation' of it, he wrote, and 'if all the letters and articles that have appeared in the newspapers on the subject were reproduced in book form they would fill a goodly volume'.

In 1881 the chairman of the South Eastern Railway (SER) visited to look over the area with a view to opening stations at West St Leonards and Ore.[2] On being shown the archway he agreed that the time had come to remodel it, and offered to pay something towards it. The borough surveyor created a design and crunched the numbers: it would cost between £6,000 and £8,000 (£600,000 and £800,000 today). Everything was going swimmingly until the railway and the council became embroiled in a legal battle about an unrelated matter, causing the archway question to be set aside.

2. The two new stations opened in 1887 and 1888 respectively.

St Andrew's Park was extensively remodelled, enlarged and improved in 1877, and in 1882 was renamed for Alexandra, Princess of Wales, on the day she and the Prince came to Hastings. For this event the town was extensively decorated and the archway bedecked with flags, garlands and a huge royal coat of arms. Putting lipstick on the pig served only to draw more attention to its ugliness. The park had cost the council thousands, and yet to reach it visitors had to traverse a stinking, murky, dangerous tunnel. Something had to be done.

For the festivities, the interior was painted; the ceiling in French grey and the walls in white. This made 'the foulness of the hole a trifle less offensive'; however, in the long term the 'objectionable eyesore' had to go. Ratepayers would have to foot the bill, but, said one local, 'Hastings people would now do anything, or give anything, almost, to be able to remove it.'

By then the problems went beyond cosmetic. Owing to the weight of the embankment above, lateral bulges and transverse cracks began to appear in the brickwork, raising fears that it might be edging towards collapse. In 1887 a reader of the *HSLO* warned that 'the equilibrium of the arch is imperilled', which may result in 'the entombment of an omnibus.' Another entreated people to 'think of the irreparable loss that might occur to this town if a crushed Councillor should be found amongst the ruins!'

In 1890 the SER offered to erect an iron bridge, provided the council paid six-sevenths of the £6,000 cost. Despite a petition bearing 986 signatures, the council voted against it. On 28th March 1891 a group of top-hatted, black-coated gentlemen was spotted surveying and measuring the archway. Despite this, two years later the 'wretched structure' was still in use and townsfolk were becoming increasingly frustrated by the lack of action. Algernon Brooker felt that newspaper editors should use their influence to press the council to demand improvements:

> If some of our local editors...would only consent to ride to their arduous duties on top of an omnibus, taking a seat on the near side, and passing through the tunnel at the same time as another vehicle is coming from the opposite direction, the result would create such widespread consternation that something would speedily be done. Of course the editors would be scalped, as to the left sides of their heads, by the brickwork of the tunnel, but there would be the pleasing consciousness of having performed a public service, and the knowledge that the loss of their ambrosial locks would be the public's gain.

In 1894 Borough Surveyor Mr Palmer drew up new plans for an elliptical arch, 40ft wide and 37ft high, constructed of red brick and terracotta. However, the SER rejected it and suggested instead a bridge similar to its magnificent three-span iron girder bridge at Folkestone. Hastings Council agreed, but when the cost of the project was revealed it had nearly doubled since 1890 to £11,700 (the equivalent to about £1.3m).

The SER would contribute 1/6th, making Hastings Council's contribution £8,113. This would be borrowed at 3% over thirty years, putting nearly £500 a year on the rates, which amounted to one-third of a penny per ratepayer.

The construction of the bridge began in June 1897. The SER's building inspector lived in London but visited at intervals. Bill Cozens, although only twenty-nine, had lately been promoted to inspector. He joined the SER from school, so had spent half his life as a bricklayer. His visit involved staying in a hotel at the seaside, so he brought his wife Maria and their two-year-old child.

About 11am on 25th August Maria took her daughter to Alexandra Park whilst Bill inspected a shaft that had been sunk into the ground to support one of the fluted columns. It was 10ft across and 65ft deep. Inside were two stages of scaffolding, one at the top and one 8ft feet from the bottom. Bill and a workman descended the ladder to the lower stage. Heavy rain had left the timber boards wet, and as Bill explained the correct way to empty a skip of runny concrete into the shaft, he slipped and was pitched forwards, falling head first onto solid concrete. The workman helped him up the ladder, and, with the assistance of others, brought him to the top. Dr Adkins was called but by the time he arrived Bill was dead. A later post mortem would show that he had fractured his skull, which, the doctor noted, was unusually thin.

A few minutes after the accident Maria saw some commotion going on at the bridge works and approached the workmen, who broke the dreadful news. At twenty-six she was a widow and her little daughter was fatherless. Tragically, by the time the bridge was finished, the little girl would also die.

In November 1898 the new bridge passed inspection and trains began to cross it. The despised archway that had blighted the road for a half-century could at long last be removed. Work began on 5th November and took three nights and three days. Jubilant locals flocked to see the demonic hole finally being abolihed and demolished and stood loitering and watching the workmen; photographers attended to capture the once-in-a-lifetime event.

Once the archway was gone locals thronged to witness the new scene. Not only could the bridge now be viewed in all its majestic glory, but also its construction allowed the roadway to be widened to nearly 50ft. The area had been transformed into one of space, light and airiness. New vistas apeared: looking north a vast expanse of sky, some pretty trees and a terrace of elegant villas opposite the park were most pleasing to the eye. Looking south one now had a clear view of the buildings on Queen's Road and of the tall townhouses of Nelson Road rising up on the West Hill above and behind them.

HSLO 30 August 1884; 29 January & 12 February 1887, 28 August 1897 and other editions too numerous to mention.

The south portal during demolition, November 1898.

The same view after the archway was removed.

5 Penrhyn Terrace, Priory Road.

Mrs Wilson received a mention in the *HSLO* of 14th April 1900. £1 1s was a guinea, and the equivalent to about £110 today.

A GRATEFUL PATIENT.—Mrs. Wilson, of 5, Penrhyn-terrace, Priory-road, Hastings, sends us a letter containing postal orders value £1 1s., with the subjoined request:—" Dear Mr. Editor,—May I venture to ask you to forward the enclosed to the Hospital at White Rock, opposite the Hastings Pier, for attention received at the time of my rather serious cycling accident. My friends will no doubt be pleased to hear that, after three weeks' acute suffering, under the skilful treatment of Dr. Harry Mansell I am progressing favourably."

1900

NEW TECHNOLOGIES

PENRHYN TERRACE

Catherine Jolliffe was born near Cardiff in 1832, the daughter of an excise officer. In 1859 she married Robert Acton Wilson, an amateur sculptor over a decade her senior. His parents ran the King's Head in Finsbury, and she lived there for a few years after Robert took over the license from his mother. By 1881 the couple had left London forever in favour of 5 Penrhyn Terrace, a new, three-bedroomed house diagonally opposite St Clement's church, Halton.

Mrs Wilson happy marriage came to an end when Robert died in 1898. She was sixty-six but had a young outlook and a bright, curious mind in a healthy, fit body. A widowhood spent in mourning was not for her; she would embrace her new life with courage and optimism. As part of this fresh start she invited her twenty-one-year-old great-niece and namesake, Catherine Jolliffe to share her comfortable home.

Young Catherine's life had been one of unremitting bereavement. Her mother was an alcoholic opium-eater and her father took his life when she and her little sister were five and three. Then her grandmother, mother and sister died, and at thirteen she ended up in an orphanage. After so much loss, so much grief, and so much insecurity, she finally found a stable, loving home with her delightful great-aunt.

In early 1900 Mrs Wilson decided to take the plunge and purchase a bicycle. They had been around for decades but were a 'male domain'. The safety bicycle, with its equal-sized wheels, chain-drive, pneumatic tyres and brakes, all of which made cycling more female-friendly, did not appear until the late 1880s. Even then, only a few of the bravest women would ride one. By the mid-1890s several manufacturers were producing models with a dropped frame to suit the female form and feminine attire.

As the new century approached growing numbers of women enjoyed the freedom the bicycle bestowed; the personal mobility was coupled with the enjoyment of physical exertion. Cycling for women became symbolic of their growing emancipation, the iconic mode of transport for the 'New Woman', one of whom stated in 1899: 'The bicycle is in truth the women's emancipator. It imparts an open-air freedom and freshness to a life hithertofore cribbed, cabined and confined by convention.'

Whilst ladies' magazines applauded the innovation the fuddy-duddies and prudes voiced their disapproval of women sitting *astride* a saddle whilst being bumped and vibrated along the rough roads.

An unknown lady with a bicycle in 1900. Mrs Wilson's bicycle and outfit would have been similar.

This cartoon depicts the fear harboured in some quarters that 'velocipedestriennes' might let their hair down, loosen their corsets, shamelessly flaunt their legs in public, smoke cigarettes like a man and ride with reckless abandon, knocking down everyone in their path.

Facing page: snippets from the *HSLO*, 1900.

THE AWFUL EFFECTS OF VELOCIPEDING.

BICYCLES FOR SALE & WANTED.

A BARGAIN.—Lady's B and A BICYCLE for immediately sale; capital condition, lady giving up riding.—Can be seen any time at 7, St. Andrew's-square, Hastings.

A BICYCLE (Lady's) and accessories for sale, in perfect condition; equal to new; B.S.A. fittings, Clincher tyres; owner giving up riding; price £7.—Can be seen at 40, Braybrooke-road, Hastings.

FOR Sale, lady's BICYCLE; Premier; cost £14 14s.; scarcely used; nickel lamp, pump, etc.; price £10 10s.—Apply 61, Warrior-square, from 2 to 4 o'clock.

CENTAUR Lady's BICYCLE; very little used; price 10 guineas.—Apply Miss Adey, 43, West-hill, St. Leonards.

LADY'S BICYCLE for sale; nearly as good as new; no further use for it; lamp, brake, pump, and wrench; price £4.—Apply 48, Southwater-road, St. Leonards.

In Hastings new machines were available from cycle depots. However, even the most up-to-date ladies' cycles were heavy, tricky to learn to ride and, the town being so hilly, they were hard work to ride anywhere other than the seafront. By 1898 secondhand cycles began to appear in the local classifieds for between £5 and £10, often described as 'rarely used' or being sold because 'owner giving up'. It seems that only the fittest and most determined women persisted with the machines. Among them was Mrs Wilson. A new machine cost about £17 (£1,700 today), a sum she could easily afford.

It took weeks, if not months, to learn to ride a bicycle; instruction books were published and training courses offered. Mrs Wilson spent the spring of 1900 practising her technique. On 21st March she was out riding alone when, two miles from home, in St Margaret's Road, St Leonards, she was hit by a sudden gust of wind and blown over. When she found she could not just get up and dust herself down, but was quite badly hurt, passers-by had her conveyed to the nearby East Sussex Hospital. She was examined briefly by the house surgeon, who said nothing was broken and sent her home to rest. She was able to get about with a stick but her injury did not get better. Dr Mansell, who lived in Collier Road, examined her and had a special boot made, which allowed her to 'hobble about'. However, he said he could not cure her injury. He suspected she had fractured her thigh but he could not confirm this.

At the time Röntgenography was prominent in the news. It was a new and miraculous diagnostic technique which used electrical vibrations to see inside the body. Discovered by Professor Röntgen in Germany in 1895, the first British demonstrations were given at St Thomas's Hospital in February 1896 and soon Röntgen rays were 'used daily by surgeons...for fixing the position of foreign substances in the living human body, or for ascertaining the deformities or fractures in bones.' Lantern slide presentations thrilled audiences with images of the insides of 'a boy who had swallowed a half-penny' and of 'a snake, a fish, a fowl, and a frog with a broken leg.' By 1898 it was asserted that, 'No medical corps attached to an army could be considered properly equipped without adequate provision of the Röntgen ray apparatus...for the speedy extraction from a wounded man of a bullet.'

But it was not all good news. In 1898 it was reported that 'Röntgen rays have very unpleasant effects on the human skin, producing more or less dangerous eruptions...dermatologists now recommend the spreading of a glutinous mixture of zinc, cinnabar, and salt of bismuth on the parts exposed.' In 1899 a French woman sued a radiographer for punitive damages for burns inflicted upon her by the rays. She sustained a wound eight inches square which caused her months of illness. During the case similar accidents were cited.

Dr Mansell asked Mrs Wilson to 'oblige him' by allowing Röntgen photographs to be taken to determine if she had a fractured thigh. Although it was expensive, she was fascinated by science and new technologies so she readily agreed. Mansell had never used them before but was told that a Mr John Blomfield was until recently the Röntgenographer at the East Sussex Hospital and had his own equipment, so he visited his studio in Robertson Street.

On 14th April the two men visited Penrhyn Terrace. Mrs Wilson was made comfortable on rugs and pillows on the floor and rays were applied to both thighs, for comparison. However, when Dr Mansell and some other medical men later examined the developed slides they were unsatisfactory, and so on 27th the men returned to Mrs Wilson for a second session. This time both hips were photographed at the same time, from the middle of her stomach.

Two weeks after the second session 'an eruption' formed across Mrs Wilson's stomach. The large, deep, serious burn, called a 'sloughing wound', was three inches across and over six inches long, with inflammation all around the edges. It caused her intense agony. After a month it had not healed. Dr Mansell passed her case to Dr Roberts, of 18 Cambridge Road. In October Dr Ticehurst also examined her; the burn had turned gangrenous and Mrs Wilson was emaciated, bedridden and semi-conscious.

Dr Harry Rosser Mansell and Joseph Harry Roberts had both graduated in 1891. Augustus Ticehurst, son of the eminent Frederick, was much older, and had qualified in 1869. Based in Charles Road, he was a consulting surgeon at the hospital and several other medical institutions and, like his father, was a JP. When these three local men failed to cure her wound, Mrs Wilson wrote personally to two London doctors: Charters James Symonds, a senior surgeon at Guy's (who was later knighted), and Nestor Tirard, a Harley Street specialist (and former Hastings resident) with a long string of impressive qualifications, who examined her in September.

Despite the attentions, advice and treatments of these five doctors, with 100 years of clinical experience between them, the horrendous wound stubbornly, and strangely, refused to heal.

Mrs Wilson's health continued to deteriorate and, despite the constant, loving care of her dear Catherine, two paid, qualified nurses tending to her round the clock and Dr Roberts on call, on 5th November she died. Dr Ticehurst performed the post mortem, and the inquest was held by Mr C. Davenport Jones at the Market Hall in George Street on 8th November,.

After her great-aunt passed away, Catherine discovered an envelope under the bedclothes in a room that had been unoccupied since September. Marked 'Not to be opened till after death', it contained a heart-rending letter in Mrs Wilson's handwriting. The letter was read out at the inquest.

> My Dear Little Treasure. The pain and anguish I suffer almost continuously from this painful sore is at times almost more than I can bear, caused by cruel over-exposure of Röntgen Rays, recommended by Mr H. Mansell, of West-hill, Hastings. It was he who engaged the photographer, Mr Blomfield, of Robertson-street, Hastings. Should anything happen to me do not grieve. My strength and nerves are so weakened and shattered with the pain I have suffered since May that if death does not speedily come I tremble to think of the consequences. God knows I have been praying for death to release me daily and hourly. If the pain does not subside — well, I cannot bear it much more. I long to rest with my dear husband in peace. My brain is all of a whirl. My blood rests upon the two men — the medical man and the photographer — who are the cause of all my cruel suffering. I sincerely thank Dr Roberts for all his kindness. He has done what he could. I pray I may retain my reason. *Catherine Wilson.*
>
> P.S. I have had the opinion of a specialist [Dr Symonds]. They never apply the X Rays more than ten minutes or a quarter of an hour. In my case these two men applied the rays for two hours to my injured leg. On April 27 two hours again. Brutal!

The *HSLO* reported the inquest and included Mrs Wilson's letter. In an extraordinary move, the editor added a *seventeen-line* footnote to explain that he published her words 'with much regret' and 'in the conviction that our readers will withhold their judgment until the whole of the evidence is before them'. 'The letter', he suggested, 'may be completely explained away'.

The coroner remarked that the case was 'rather peculiar'. He adjourned the inquest to give time for the doctor and the photographer to prepare their defence against the allegation that they had caused Mrs Wilson's death, and for her side to collect evidence of any 'neglect or improper usage'.

THE RONTGEN RAYS CASE.

ADJOURNED INQUEST YESTERDAY.

FULL HISTORY OF THE AFFAIR.

THE TIME OF THE EXPOSURE.

ST. BARTHOLOMEW'S HOSPITAL EXPERT'S VIEWS.

DR. H. R MANSELL & MR. BLOMFIELD GIVE EVIDENCE.

WHOLLY EXONERATED BY THE JURY.

VERDICT RECEIVED WITH LOUD APPLAUSE.

X-Ray Dangers.

LONG EXPOSURE IN THE HASTINGS CASE.

THE DANGERS OF THE RONTGEN RAYS.

STRANGE STATEMENTS AT AN INQUEST.

ALLEGED TORTURE BY X-RAYS.

SENSATIONAL CASE.

TREATMENT BY MEANS OF X-RAYS.
ALLEGED FATAL EFFECTS.

THE RONTGEN RAYS

DO THEY CAUSE DEATH?

EXTRAORDINARY STATEMENTS AT HASTINGS.

FATAL BICYCLE ACCIDENT.

RONTGEN RAYS DENOUNCED.

ALLEGED FATAL EFFECTS OF X RAYS.

RONTGEN RAYS AND DEATH.
AN EXTRAORDINARY CASE.

The inquest was resumed at the town hall on 16th November and lasted four-and-a-half hours. Each party brought a solicitor, and Catherine had also engaged a London barrister. Chief Constable C.F. Baker attended, with a sergeant, doubtless in case anything criminal was revealed.

Catherine, who had been present at both applications of the Röntgen rays, told the court that Dr Mansell visited with Mr Blomfield but left the room whilst the rays were applied. She did not make any record of how long it took, but Mrs Wilson did. The subsequent eruption of the burn prompted her to tell Catherine that the first application had lasted two hours and the second two hours and ten minutes. Mr Blomfield trenchantly denied this and Dr Mansell supported him. He had applied the rays for thirty-five minutes during the first session and forty-five the second. On each occasion, although he was at the house for two-and-a-half hours, more than half of that time was expended in setting up and dismantling the equipment.

Dr Lewis Jones of St Bartholomew's Hospital said that the use of the rays had been correct. He had examined Mr Blomfield's apparatus, which had cost a whopping £100 (£10,000 today). Whilst it was true that it was eighteen months out of date, this was because the new technology was being updated so frequently. It was not reasonable to expect every provincial photographer to suffer the expense of buying new equipment every few months. The later machines were much more powerful and the rays could therefore be applied for shorter times, but the setup Mr Blomfield used had been widely in use until recently, with no ill effects.

The court heard that, as poor Mrs Wilson became increasingly ground down, distressed and depressed by the unending, excruciating pain from the wound, she reached the point where she felt her life not worth living. She said that she had lost her appetite and, in the final five weeks of her life, refused food. The two nurses even resorted to attempting to force-feed her.

Dr Roberts told the court that the wound was caused by the Röntgen rays. In his opinion Mrs Wilson died from exhaustion and from the effects of shock caused by the fracture of the thigh and the Röntgen rays.

The jurymen accepted part of Dr Roberts's opinion, but dismissed Mrs Wilson's assertion from the grave that the rays were applied for too long. They decided on a verdict of 'death from shock and exhaustion and the effect of Röntgen rays on an already weakened system', but made a special point of stating that no blame was attached to either the doctor or the photographer. Upon hearing this, a group of spectators cheered and applauded. Both men were well known and had many clients as well as relations living locally. Other than Catherine, her 'dear little treasure', Mrs Wilson had no one to root for her.

The HSLO report filled more column-inches than I have ever seen devoted to one death. It took up three and three-quarter columns of the broadsheet, totalling over 6,500 words, plus the report of the first session ran to 1,200 words. Brief summaries of the inquest appeared in over forty newspapers country-wide and carried some startling headlines (see facing page).

DIGRESSION: JOHN HENRY BLOMFIELD

John's mother Elizabeth Eldridge was born in Hastings. In August 1840, aged seventeen, she travelled to Lewes to hear a touring speaker, the Rev Mr Knibb, describe his philanthropic and educational work as a Baptist missionary in Jamaica. The slaves had recently been freed and he had devoted his life to helping them. The Missionary Society needed more teachers, and Elizabeth and her Londoner friend Henry Blomfield volunteered. However, upon discovering that single women were not permitted to go, they married at the Croft Chapel in Gloucester Place and sailed to Jamaica where they taught at missionary schools.

Returning to England in 1849 their children became the only Jamaican-born people living in New Romney, where Henry was a Baptist minister. John was born in 1850, and in 1856 the family moved permanently to Hastings, where they opened a boarding school and added five more children to their brood.

John grew up to be a prominent local photographer, operating between 1867 and 1928 at 44 Robertson Street, the most fashionable street in town. Among his customers were the Prince of Wales, the Duke and Duchess of Teck, Earl de la Warr, Lady Anna and Lord Thomas Brassey MP and William Lucas Shadwell MP. In 1888 he co-founded the Hastings & St Leonards Photographic Society, whose president was Wilson Noble, then MP for Hastings.

John embraced every innovation in his trade; he pioneered novel formats and introduced new technology such as electric lighting in the 1880s and Röntgen ray photography in the late 1890s.

In June 1898 John's thirteen-year-old son Jack had a 'strange exit': he was hit in the chest by a cricket ball during batting practice on Priory Meadow. The impact caused his heart to stop. Despite the administration of artificial respiration and rum-and-brandy, the poor little boy expired on the spot. A large crowd gathered outside the family's home, 41 Wellington Square, to express their sorrow at the tragedy and to watch the horse-drawn, glass-sided hearse convey his coffin to St Mary-in-the-Castle for the service and thence to the Borough Cemetery.

PORTRAITS PAINTED
ARTISTIC PHOTOGRAPHS
& ENLARGEMENTS

Mr
J. H. BLOMFIELD

TRINITY HOUSE
44, Robertson Street
HASTINGS

In his 'Flotsam and Jetsam' column, the editor of the *HSLO* almost gloated when he referred to his previous week's footnote:

How amply warranted I was in making that appeal the verdict given yesterday attests. The Jury, after one of the most protracted and painstaking investigations that have ever taken place in the local Coroner's Court, found that no blame whatever attached to the medical man or the photographer.

On 19th November, having read about the case in the London papers in his Sloane Street townhouse, Wilson Noble, who had been MP for Hastings from 1886 until 1895, and was president of the local photographic club co-founded by Mr Blomfield, wrote to the *HSLO*. He was worried that 'some might be inclined to suppose that a danger exists in the use of these valuable aids to diagnosis.' Because the rays were now stronger, they could be applied for less time, and so no longer burned the skin. 'It would be a thousand pities', he opined, if people refused the rays just because of Mrs Wilson's case.

The Röntgen rays did kill Mrs Wilson, albeit indirectly. She could no longer bear the mental or physical torture of suffering six months of excruciating agony from the horrific skin burn caused by the rays. What the doctors termed 'exhaustion' was in reality a severe lack of nutrition, caused by Mrs Wilson herself. She was utterly desperate to be released from her living hell, but being bedridden had no way to obtain a drug or weapon with which to end her life. She resorted to the only means open to her: self-starvation, and thus died by her own hand.

After her death, reports of similar severe burn wounds appeared in the papers. In the worst case the head of the Röntgen Department at Vienna General Hospital was ordered to pay £1,500 damages (£150,000 today) for giving a patient an overdose of rays in 1902. He was so badly burned that he almost lost his life and had to lie in bed for a year.

Catherine inherited her great-aunt's estate, which amounted to £3,080 (about £335,000 today). She left Hastings, married a drugstore proprietor in 1905, raised a family and seems to have led a normal, happy life. She died in 1950.

Professor Röntgen was awarded the first Nobel Prize for Physics in 1901. Eschewing fame, honours or fortune, he refused a title and donated the prize money to his university. Sadly the First World War wiped out his pension and savings and left him bankrupt and pfennigless. He had humbly insisted that his invention not carry his name but instead be called 'x rays'.

References: *The People* 4 March 1883; *London Evening Standard* 30 June 1898; *Dundee Courier* 1 December 1899; *HSLO* 10, 17 & 24 November 1900; *Sevenoaks Chronicle* 21 December 1900; *Edinburgh Evening News* 30 August 1902; New woman quote, *Guardian* 9 June 2015.

The pier in 1904, the week that 'The Ring that Binds' was playing at the pavilion, the interior of which is pictured below. The 50ft corridor must have run parallel to the auditorium.

The Nineteenth Click

Hastings Pier

Hastings Pier was designed by Eugenius Birch who, having spent time in India, made its tollhouses octagonal and gave the pavilion onion domes and tall finials. With a capacity of 2,000, from its opening in 1872 it was the biggest function room in the borough.

In 1879 actor-comedian Johnny Hunter was appointed entertainment manager at £20 a week, and would hold the post for thirty years.[1] He created a resident orchestra and a theatre company and also booked a wide range of outside acts, including gipsy violinists, light opera, solo vocalists, child musical prodigies, choirs, virtuoso pianists, brass bands and stand-up comedians. His job was his whole life: he even married one of the resident singers, Florence Bayley, with whom he lived close to the pier at 18 White Rock.

Johnny hired a number of theatre hands. One, Charles Tubbs, had worked on the pier since 1872. As a boy he started as a toll collector, then after working as a scene-shifter in the pavilion eventually became the stage carpenter, creating the scenery and some props. If needed he would step in and play a small role, such as that of Inspector Thickhead in 1894. He was better known as a yachtsman, regatta official and champion rower who won countless trophies and designed and built a famous, prize-winning sailing boat called the *Donovan*. Despite being so busy he found the time and energy to make his wife pregnant at least twelve times, though sadly seven of their offspring died in childhood.

His son Ernie, born in 1881, was a chip off the old carpenter's block. He rowed in singles, pairs and fours, was junior south coast sculling champion, and he won the Cinque Port Rowing Club's du Cros Challenge Cup. The instant he left school he joined his father at the pavilion, where he was a stage hand and a bit-part actor; some years later his sister joined them as wardrobe mistress.

Another long-serving member of Johnny's team was Charlie Christian, the assistant stage carpenter, scene-shifter and stage extra. Born in Swan Yard on 27th April 1871, twenty-five days too late to be included in the census, his mother was a nurse and his father was an ostler at the Swan Hotel, and later a fly driver.[2] Charles started work on the pier as a teenage stage hand. He married Annie Skinner in 1894 and by 1904 they had four children.

1. Between 1908 and 1924 he was also the piermaster.
2. When Charlie was a baby his father 'Jack' Christian was summonsed several times for petty offences. He was handy with his fists and once assaulted a colleague during an argument in the Swan Yard, just like Walker in 'The Pitchforked Postilion'.

Johnny Hunter excelled at giving the people what they wanted, and the grateful public flocked to the pier in their tens of thousands to enjoy his offerings. In 1905 for example, 'large and enthusiastic audiences' crowded into the pavilion twice daily to view a pictorial display about 'Our Army and Navy', and the melodrama 'Dare Devil Dorothy' played to a full house nightly. In winter every performance of the plays 'Hand in Glove' and 'East Lynne' was well attended. In the summer of 1906 the pavilion was 'packed almost to suffocation', even on a Tuesday, when top-class music hall comedians George Robey and Albert Chevalier gave flying matinée performances. A drama starring actress Go-Won-Go-Mohawk drew crowds who had never before seen a 'Red Indian'. In late November the Pier Dramatic Society staged an American drama called 'The Danites'. The play was set in the Far West during the Gold Rush. In December Johnny produced his twenty-eighth panto (he was always the dame) and organised a Christmas Day concert.

In 'The Danites' two characters brandished guns, and one was fired at the character George, played by Charlie Christian. Two revolvers were provided by the props department: one was a dummy and the other held one blank cartridge. After the final performance on 1st December it was Ernie Tubbs's job to return them to their cases and lock them safely away. The property manager said he had the loaded one, so Ernie looked for the dummy, which he found in a dressing basket. As he carried it behind his back along a 50ft corridor to Dressing Room 7, he idly clicked the trigger (what must have been) nineteen times.[3] He was still clicking it as he entered the room, which was filled with cast and crew packing up and getting ready to leave. Charlie Christian, who was sitting on a large wicker hamper, suddenly shrieked 'Oh! My leg!' The revolver has unexpectedly fired a blank cartridge, and he was hit in the right thigh from a distance of eighteen inches.

Ernie was horrified. Ridden with guilt he carried Charlie on his back down two flights of stairs, placed him on a truck and rolled him the length of the pier to the East Sussex Hospital, which stood opposite. The wound, which was blackened from a gunpowder burn, was treated by the Bombay-born assistant honorary surgeon Maneckji Pirozsaw Kerrawalla, who had recently qualified from Brussels and Glasgow medical schools. He cut off the burned, black edges of the hole and applied a fomentation of antiseptic.

Ernie took Charlie home in a carriage. He was filled with remorse at inflicting such an injury on someone, especially Charlie, who had been a good friend and colleague for fourteen years. How ghastly he must have felt handing Charlie over to his wife.

3. The blank cartridge would have been loaded into the first chamber, so that during the play it would fire at the first pull of the trigger. However, it was malfunctioning. Clearly the blasting cap was not being struck by the firing pin. Repeatedly pulling the trigger gave another chance for the pin to strike every fifth pull. Therefore, it must have failed to fire when pulled on stage, and Ernie must have pulled the trigger four times to land on the blank-filled chamber again, and thence every fifth pull. He guessed he pulled it about twenty times; it was actually nineteen.

Under the loving care of his wife and his mother, Charlie initially progressed satisfactorily, and for nearly a week he travelled daily by tram from 8 St George's Road to the hospital to have the dressing changed and the wound inspected. But one night he suddenly felt very ill. Dr Mansell suspected blood poisoning and tetanus. Charlie was admitted to hospital, where three more doctors examined him. On Saturday 15th December the *HSLO* reported that he was in 'an exceedingly grave condition', and on Monday morning he died. He was just thirty-five.

Deputy Coroner W.J. Glenister held an inquest at the hospital. Mr Weston (secretary to the pier company) and Johnny Hunter attended. Witnesses said that the revolver in question was defective and some nights failed to fire, although nobody had reported it. Revolvers had been used on that stage for twenty-eight years and this was the first mishap. Ernie explained in detail what happened, and the coroner expressed dismay that 'the lesson that people should not toy or trifle with firearms would never be learnt'. The jurymen returned a verdict of 'death by misadventure'. No blame was placed on Ernie, but they recommended that the defective weapon 'be done away with'. Everyone expressed sympathy with the widow and Mr Weston said that everything possible would be done for her 'in a monetary sense'.

The funeral took place the next day at the Borough Cemetery. It was just before Christmas and bitterly cold. Those present included Annie, her two elder children, aged ten and eight, Charlie's mother and brother, Ernie and his father and some other pier staff. One of the pallbearers was future Piermaster Teddy Down, predecessor to Eric Mumford, who would also meet with a tragic end on the pier (see Volume One).

Poor Annie was left to explain to her children, the youngest of which was only four, why they would never see their daddy again. Johnny Hunter started a fund for them, and placed a collection box in the West Tollhouse. Among the early contributors were the sitting MP Harvey du Cros (£2 2s), Piermaster Turner (15s) and Ernie Tubbs (5s). Spectators at a football match gave a total of £2 16s to a collector, as did the staff of the Gaiety Theatre. The total amount collected was not published. Annie became a cook and her elder son worked in a newsagent. They lived at 106 St George's Road, with the two younger children and her late husband's mother.

Earlier in 1906 the *HSLO* had run an article lauding Johnny Hunter for providing superb entertainment for twenty-seven years, which drew the public to visit the pier. In the busiest year, 1891, the number of visitors passing through the toll booths was 768,182. The article praised his 'long and uninterrupted run of success', remarking that he 'came, saw and conquered' Hastings and 'continues to hold his own splendidly'. It ended with the wish: 'Long may he reign!' However, less than four years later the directors terminated his contract, much to the shock and dismay of many fans, who inundated the local press with protest letters.

A year after the shooting accident Ernie Tubbs married Mabel Haste, one of the amateur players on the pavilion stage. The couple had two children.

One freezing cold night in February 1910, when his first child was just four days old, Ernie and his father became local heroes.

SENSATIONAL RESCUE. STARTLING OCCURRENCE AT HASTINGS PIER.

On Monday night, about nine o'clock, Mrs Florence Woolland, visiting Hastings for the benefit of her health, was walking on the deck with a nurse when she suddenly ran to the side of the pier and jumped into the sea. Three members of the Rowing Club — Charles Tubbs, his son Ernest, and Teddy Down — launched the pier boat from the davits under the pavilion deck. By the exercise of much skill and perseverance Messrs Tubbs somehow kept the boat afloat, notwithstanding the heavy sea, and rescued the lady. The management of the pier deserve credit for the promptitude with which they acted.

From an eye-witness, it appears that the rescue was almost miraculous, and a much more courageous affair than might be imagined from the modesty of the three chief actors. In the first instance, the nurse gave the alarm at the tollhouse, and from thence the news was telephoned to the authorities in the pavilion. Mr Hawker communicated the alarm to the employees, including Ernest, who was working the mechanical effects on the stage. He and his father lowered the boat into the water and launched it. Mr Down watched from above, and shouted directions to Charles, who was in the boat searching for the lady whilst his son manned the oars. There was a very heavy sea, and nothing could be seen by those in the boat, except in their own immediate vicinity. The lady fell from the westward (the windward) side of the pier, and was drifting towards the Baths. A small patch of black clothing was spotted by the rescuers, then Charles saw the lady's head bobbing above the surface, her clothing had kept her afloat. Ernest rowed towards her and together they lifted her into the boat. This was the most critical time, for with both men in the stern the heavy sea was coming into the craft. Fortunately for herself and her rescuers, the lady was unconscious. Had it been otherwise, the natural instinct to struggle would probably have ended with the boat being capsized, and all three losing their lives.

It was impossible to go ashore, owing to the surf, and the only thing to be done was to return to the pier and raise the boat to the davits. The lady was carried out and placed on a truck which had been hastily procured, and wheeled down the pier towards the gates. John Hunter, while the rescue was in progress, telephoned the hospital for an ambulance. Half-way along the hospital stretcher met the rescuing party, and the lady was transferred. Some idea of the rapidity of the rescue may be formed from the fact that eye-witnesses state that only eight minutes elapsed between the first alarm and the arrival of the rescued lady at the hospital. The lady is now making satisfactory progress.

Perhaps it was fitting that Fate gave Ernie the opportunity to save a life to atone for the life he accidentally ended.

Although they remained working on the pier, over the next five years Charles and Ernie both changed trade; the father became an engineer and the son an electrician. In addition, Ernie joined the Hastings Borough Volunteer Fire Brigade, giving him more opportunities to save lives.

When the First World War began in 1914 Ernie was thirty-three and so he did not get called up at that time. However, three years later, in April 1917, to serve his King and Country he left his wife and children at home at 16 Linton Terrace and joined the Royal Field Artillery as a gunner. After six months training and deployment in England, his battalion was sent to France.

On 15th July 1917 the Hastings Pier Pavilion was completely destroyed by fire. Charles Tubbs lost all his tools, collected during his forty-four years at the pier and worth £60 (£6,000 today). The editor of the *HSLO* and Johnny Hunter organised a collection for him and by September they were able to present him with £29 17s (£1,700 today).

Just eight weeks later, on 18th October, Ernie was killed in action in Flanders. Just like Charlie Christian's children, his son and daughter, then six and seven, would grow up without their dad.

References: *HSLO* 13 October & 22 December 1906 and 12 February 1910; *Sussex Express* 22 December 1906; www.hastingspierarchive.org.uk

A scene familiar to everyone in this chapter: the pier with its onion domes and finials, yachts, ornate gas lamps, bath-chair men touting for business and posters advertising forthcoming performances and boat trip timetables.

MAJOR F. FREEMAN-THOMAS, JR. AND THE HON. MRS. FREEMAN-THOMAS
BEING INTRODUCED BY MR. GABB TO THE CAPT. OF THE
HASTINGS F.C. JANUARY 13TH, 1908.   JUDGE-PHOTO

ENGLISH CUP TIE
HASTINGS v PORTSMOUTH
JAN 11 08

Judge's photographs of Hastings United playing at Priory Meadow in January 1908. The team was formed in 1906 from a merger of Hastings (founded 1889) and St Leonards (1898).

The top picture looks east; South Terrace can be seen in the background. The team was being introduced to Major Freeman Freeman-Thomas and his wife, the Hon. Marie, daughter of Thomas Brassey. After serving as Liberal MP for Hastings 1900–1906 and secretary to Prime Minister Asquith in 1910 Mr Thomas became Baron Willingdon.

The lower photo looks south-east; the Bedford Hotel is in the centre, on the corner of Portland Place. The photos come from the Cyril Clarke collection, which he left to his niece Paula Monk, who lent them to Leon Pettit, owner of hastingsfootballhistory.co.uk, who very kindly sent copies to me. Thanks to everyone in that chain.

1909

LINESMAN ON THE LINE

ORE TUNNEL

Like his father, Edward Keene was an engine fitter at the railway locomotive workshops at Ashford. He joined the works' South Eastern Rangers football team at its birth in 1881, and was soon being name-checked in the local press as an impressive centre-forward. In 1889, as captain, he scored all three goals — the third being a stonking header — against Kentish Express, with whom his team soon merged to become Ashford United. It lost its first FA Cup match 6–2, and was pulverised by Woolwich Arsenal in an FA Cup qualifying match, losing 12–0. Under his captaincy the team won the Kent Cup three times.

By the age of twenty-five Edward was nick-named 'Daddy Keene', maybe he was the only player with offspring; he and his wife (the foreman's daughter) had a baby son, Percy.

When Keene left the team in 1894 a reporter dubbed him 'the hero of a hundred fights, without whom the Ashford team seems incomplete'. He did not leave the beautiful game; from 1896 he was a referee and linesman in Sussex and Kent, and soon became a familiar face in Hastings.

On Saturday 23rd October 1909 he travelled to Hastings to be a linesman at Priory Meadow for a game between Hastings and St Leonards United and the Woolwich Arsenal Reserves. Whilst here he sent a postcard to a Folkestone club, confirming he would referee its own match against the Reserves on 27th. After the visiting team beat Hastings 3–2 Keene made his way back to the station, where Bill Andrews, a middle-aged ticket collector and football fan, walked him to his train as the pair discussed the match. Choosing an empty single compartment Keene placed his belongings on the seat and at 6.10pm the pair said their goodbyes. Andrews closed and secured the door, and the train pulled away en route to Ashford.

At Rye, the next stop, a Gladstone bag, a gentleman's walking-stick, a smart hat and a newspaper were found abandoned in an empty compartment. Thinking a man had put them on the train and been left behind when it departed, Guard Albert Reeve took them with him to Ashford and then back to Hastings. When nobody claimed them two mature men, James Crittenden, a ganger-platelayer who lived at 8 Hurrell Road, and Police Sergeant John Dudeney, of 174 Hughenden Road, were instructed by the station master to search the line. Setting out from Hastings at 9pm with an oil lamp each to illuminate the track ahead, they walked eastwards along the permanent way and through Mount Pleasant Tunnel towards Ore.

MANY RAILWAY MYSTERIES.

Well-Known Football Official Found Dead on the Line.

A SERIES of mysterious train incidents—no fewer than four in number—are engaging the attention of the police and railway authorities in various parts of the country.

Mr. Keene, the well-known football referee in Sussex, who resides at Beaver Road, Ashford, had acted as linesman on Saturday in the South-Eastern League game between Woolwich Arsenal and Hastings United at Hastings.

In the absence of an image of Daddy Keene, here is a drawing of Mark Tapley, drawn in Hastings in 1910 by Harry Furniss, who lived and died at 8 High Wickham.

Above: *Illustrated Police News* 30 October 1909; below: *HSLO* 30 October 1909.

A TRAGIC AFTERMATH TO SATURDAY'S MATCH.

Little did the many who noticed "Daddy" Keene's pleasant smile on the "line" at Saturday's match, and those who exchanged the usual greetings with him, imagine that they had seen that cheery countenance and heard that familiar voice for the last time. But so it was, for the Sunday papers recorded the dreadful accident that has deprived us all of an old friend. "Daddy" was an institution in Sussex football, and general and deep sympathy will be extended to his closer relations by many thousands who had grown to know his "Mark Tapley" personality on the football field. E. J. Keene, who was born and lived at Ashford, played in his time for South-Eastern Rangers, Ashford United, Hampstead, Hotspurs (when at Wimbledon) and also toured in Belgium with Tunbridge Wells. He played eight years in succession for Kent County as centre-forward, gaining both County Badge and Cap. He started to referee in 1896, and had taken charge of Football Association Cup-ties, London Cup-ties, Kent finals, County matches, Eastbourne Charity Cup Finals Kent League, and Southern League matches.

At 10pm, about sixty feet into Ore Tunnel, they found a dead body on the up line between the outer rail and the side wall. High up on the mouth of the tunnel a small piece of brickwork had been chipped off and some hair and blood were stuck to it. The man's pockets held a gold watch and chain and just over seven shillings (about £40 today). On the back of his head was the most ghastly, deep gash, a good four inches long. Police Surgeon Adolphus T. Field would later confirm that death was due to a fractured skull.

The inquest was held by W.J. Glenister at Ore Schools on 27th October. As well as the wtnesses, a senior official of the South Eastern & Chatham Railway, Chief Constable Frederick James, the referee of the match and Mrs Isabella Keene were present. Suicide was ruled out: Keene was a jolly, cheerful soul with a steady career, a fulfilling hobby, a loving wife and, of their four children, the youngest was just four years old. Foul play was impossible: he was the sole occupant of the compartment and Rye was the first stop.

Railway officials explained that the distance from the carriage window to the brick lining of the tunnel at the point Mr Keene's head collided with it was 17 inches. A man of his height would be too short have hit the mouth of the tunnel with his head at the point where the brickwork was damaged just by leaning out. Marks from muddy boots on the upholstery showed that he had placed one foot on each facing seat and leaned out of the window whilst standing almost upright.

Why did Keene do something so stupidly dangerous? He was an intelligent, sensible, responsible and mature railwayman of forty-four who had recently been promoted to foreman of engine fitters. He travelled by rail constantly and must have known there were tunnels on that line, as there were on almost every line he used. One railwayman wondered if maybe Keene was trying to peer into the next compartment.

A verdict of 'accidental death' was returned, the jury adding that the SECR should fit a horizontal bar halfway up every window to prevent passengers from leaning out.

News of Keene's tragic death was covered by more than two dozen papers (some mistakenly stated that Keene had refereed the match, whilst others called it the 'Kent Tunnel Mystery'). The Canterbury Journal lauded him as 'a player of more than ordinary repute' and 'one of the most respected referees in Kent'.

Hastings United rose to the top of the Division Two B of the Southern League, only to be hammered by Stoke 6–0. Sadly, the club folded in mid-1910 owing to financial problems and a failure to gain promotion.

When Daddy Keene died, his son Percy had already followed him into the locomotive works, as an apprentice brass turner. Ashford United had disbanded in 1907, but in 1910 he joined a new club called Ashford Railway Works, and soon became a noted centre-forward. Sadly, his father did not live to see Percy bought by Crystal Palace in 1912.

References: HSLO and Canterbury Journal, both 30 October 1909.

Two photographic portraits of Ghita in 1903. *Left*, looking determined and serious. *Below*, cat-balancing in a beaded gown of black satin and voile.

BEDSTEAD & BOOTLACE

BREDE PLACE

Ghita Stanhope was born into wealth and privilege, and had advantages, and opportunities that poorer girls could only daydream about. She had no need to earn her living: a luxury lifestyle was hers for the taking.

Her mother's father was the 6th Baron Vernon; her father, the Hon. H.A. Stanhope, was a son of the 5th Earl Stanhope. He was a clergyman, and when Gertrude was born on 26th November 1881 he conducted her baptism, writing his name in the register as the father and signing it as the rector. His brother inherited the earldom and passed it to his son, and so Gertrude was cousin to the 6th Earl Stanhope. As she grew up she asked people to call her 'Ghita'.

During Ghita's childhood her family lived in a succession of grand townhouses in the most fashionable and expensive areas of London. In the 1911 census their sixteen-room household in Belgravia consisted of parents and two adult daughters, looked after by eight residential servants. It was just like the popular 1970s TV series 'Upstairs, Downstairs'. She and her sisters were educated by a residential governess and private tutors, and then sent to a finishing school in Switzerland. Throughout their lives servants did everything for them; they never once had to cook a meal, sweep a floor, answer the front door or even brush their own hair.

Girls of Ghita's social standing were raised, trained and groomed to be the worthy wives and society hostesses of aristocrats, diplomats and politicians. She was among the upper set's most eligible bachelorettes: beautiful, elegant, accomplished, intelligent and from one of the best families.

After being launched into society at a debutante's ball in 1902, gossip-columnists reported on her appearance at glittering receptions, boxes at the theatre, charity balls and upper-crust weddings, where she was in demand as a bridesmaid. Her delicate satin, lace or taffeta gowns were ornamented by the family diamonds and pearls and matched with luxurious fur stoles. She enjoyed weekends at friends' country houses, went shooting and hunting and attended race meetings. Everyone in her circle either had a title or were landed gentry, and her name appeared frequently in posh periodicals, including the *Tatler*, the *Gentlewoman* and the *Bystander*.

The Rye-based author Henry James called Ghita 'the most charming young thing conceivable'; another observer praised her 'attractive personality', which made her 'everywhere an all-round favourite'. She 'carried about her a slight reminiscence of the bearing of a girl of the early Victorian period, a dainty quaintness and gentleness, very refreshing in this day of brusquerie, and often of forwardness.' But looks can and do deceive. Ghita was no shrinking violet; she was fiercely independent and, just as she rejected her birth name, so she declined to marry. She also broke with convention by taking on serious academic endeavours, including penning an article on socialism for the *Westminster Review* in 1908. More ambitiously, she embarked on a biography of her great-great-grandfather, the 3rd Earl Stanhope, a scientist, engineer, inventor and statesman, educating herself on the subject of early marine engineering in order to recount her kinsman's succcessful experiments in that field. At the time this was not considered to be a fitting subject for any girl to study, let alone an upper-class debutante, who was expected to fill her head with frippery, lightweight, 'feminine' pursuits, and the search for a suitable husband.

In 1910 Ghita was the chief bridesmaid at the wedding of her close friend Clare Frewen to Wilfred Sheridan. Shortly afterwards Ghita's mother became very ill, and for two years Ghita was largely absent from the social whirl whilst she nursed her. Although the servants did the practical work the worry and stress took its toll. Ghita adored her mother and her nerves broke down under the strain of seeing her suffer. Friends were concerned that a sleeping draught her doctor prescribed for insomnia was far too strong and adversely affected her mind and nerves. Although she would be an invalid for the rest of her days, her mother improved sufficiently for Ghita to return to her normal life.

In September 1912 Ghita she accepted an invitation to get away from the hustle and bustle of London and stay awhile with Clare Sheridan's parents at their country home, Brede Place, a twenty-room, fourteenth-century manor with stone-mullioned windows, oak panelling, pointed Gothic doors and a private chapel. Her hosts were Moreton and Clara Frewen. He was an adventurer who had earned himself the derogatory nickname 'Mortal Ruin'; his wife was a wealthy New Yorker whose nephew was the MP Winston Churchill.

When Ghita arrived at Brede she was in good spirits. During the first weekend she accompanied a shooting party, which ensured she had plenty of invigorating country air and a very long and hearty walk. The next day, Monday 9th September, was Clare's birthday. Since her marriage she had lived at Mitchen Hall, a manor house out in the sticks near Godalming. She was throwing a huge house-party and of course her parents were attending. They fully expected to take Ghita along, but in 1912 even top-of-the-range motor cars were slow and uncomfortable. As much as she wanted to see Clare, Ghita did not feel up to the gruelling ordeal of a 160-mile road trip, even though they could stay overnight and return the next day.

On Monday morning the Frewens set off without Ghita, leaving her in the house with her own lady's maid as well as their residential servants. That afternoon Ghita told Mrs Dames, the housekeeper, that she might go to tea at nearby Brickwall, the magnificent country seat residence of Moreton's brother, Colonel Frewen, situated near Northiam. 'If I should not go, don't trouble about tea unless I ring', she said. When she did not ring, nor make an appearance for several hours, Mrs Dames became concerned and went up to her room. She was not there, yet her hat and coat were still on the peg downstairs.

A housemaid discovered that the door of an unused bedroom had been locked from the inside. She called Mrs Dames, who knocked and called out 'Miss Stanhope'. No sound came from within, so she summoned her husband George, the resident caretaker. He and a male visitor went around to another door to the room, which had been screwed shut, and gained entry.

Ghita lay on the floor, motionless and with the most horrific injury. The top of her head had been blown off and there was blood everywhere. A double-barrelled shotgun was tied to the bottom rail of the brass bedstead. Dr Skinner and P.C. Pullen were summoned. Together the pair examined the scene. Ghita had knotted two bootlaces together, tied one end onto the trigger and the other onto the bed rail, and looped the bootlace around her foot. She then sat on a chair, placed the barrel of the shotgun in her mouth, and moved her foot to tug on the bootlace, which pulled the trigger. Simple, ingenious and effective.

An inquest was held in the chapel at Brede Place by coroner Charles Sheppard, The public were barred and there was no jury. In a letter to her sister, found in her room, she had written: 'My head does still feel so funny. I don't know what I am doing half the time. I don't know what it is or why. No one would believe how odd I feel — I feel so odd and irresponsible. I don't know why.' Sheppard returned a verdict of 'suicide whilst of unsound mind'. No blame was place on the doctor who prescribed the drugs that damaged her mind. The few press reports were brief and made no mention of where Ghita's lady's maid was whilst she was preparing to kill herself, nor how she had so easily obtained access to a shotgun and ammunition, which should have been under lock and key, without any member of staff seeing her.

A Hastings undertaker, Plummer Roddis, sent their special motor hearse to convey Ghita's coffin to her cousin Earl Stanhope's country seat, Chevening, in Kent. Her body lay overnight in the chapel before being laid to rest in the family's exclusive, railed-in enclosure within the village churchyard. At the funeral were estate staff, parishioners and servants but few friends. The local press listed who attended and who sent flowers; Clare Sheridan did neither. The HSLO did not publish a report her death or inquest; it mentioned only the funeral, and that was tucked away at the foot of the fourth column of page eight.

Soon after her death the writer Henry James, a friend of the Frewens, referred to 'Little Ghita Stanhope', who 'blew her brains out in the most gruesome way'. He called her 'frankly demented', a cruel comment and a dismissive insult against an intelligent, kind woman driven to suicide by the long term stress of caring for her mother, and a mind affected by prescribed drugs.

The biography Ghita was writing, *The Life of Charles, Third Earl Stanhope*, was revised and completed by G.P. Gooch and published by Longmans in 1914.

References: *Whitstable Times* 21 September 1912; *Sussex Agricultural Express* 13 September 1912; *The Bystander* 18 September 1912; *The Sketch* 24 July 1946.

Clare Sheridan in the grounds of Brede Place in the 1940s. She led a most extraordinary life; readers are urged to read the comprehensive page about her on Wikipedia, or purchase of a copy of Betty Taylor's book *Clare Sheridan* from the Hastings Press.

The *Illustrated Police News* artist's impression of the scene of the tragedy at Brede Place.

LADY'S DETERMINED SUICIDE NEAR HASTINGS.

1914

SCARED TO DEATH

CLIVE AVENUE

German-born Hugo Krebs emigrated to London in 1872, when he was a lad of twenty. Back home, his father was an innkeeper, which is doubtless how he learned the catering trade. After a few years of hard work and dedication he became the owner of a popular dining room in fashionable Marylebone. A genteel and yet humble man, Hugo ran his business impeccably and seems in every way to have been a fine and upstanding citizen.

In 1882 he married Alice Brown, the daughter of a Croydon builder who likely moved to London for work, possibly at Hugo's establishment. The couple had no children, but dedicated themselves entirely to each other, their customers and their business. Together they acquired and ran an elegant boutique hotel close to St James's Palace, and later opened an upmarket eating-house in Heddon Street, Piccadilly (now the location of Gordon Ramsay's flagship restaurant).

In 1911, after decades of toil, the couple sold the restaurant and gave up their flat in Kensington and retired to Hastings. With their hard-earning savings they were able to purchase 25 Clive Avenue, a delightfully neat and new six-roomed, bay-windowed semi, which they furnished and fitted up to their taste to be their 'forever home'.

But retirement was not the dream life Hugo imagined: he missed the hustle-bustle of running a busy London establishment, the constant human interaction, the difficult but gratifying work of striving to keep his esteemed guests and diners comfortable and satisfied. He felt rather depressed at times. When, in the summer of 1914, Britain went to war with Germany Hugo was, understandably, deeply upset. He had lived here for forty of his sixty-two years and felt English, not German. But one's birthplace always takes a special place in a sentimental heart, and his was broken to see the two countries at war.

All Germans were ordered to register at their local police station. Mr Krebs duly complied, then returned to pottering in his garden and other harmless and wholesome retirement activities.

At 9am on Saturday 7th November there was a rap on the door. It was Police Sub-inspector Janes. He had come to inform them that Hastings had been designated a 'Prohibited Area'. An order dated 2nd November required 'aliens' to leave Hastings within four days, or to apply to the Chief Constable to get permission to remain. There were, Janes remarked sternly, posters displayed all over the town. Neither Hugo nor Alice had seen them, because they seldom went into town. Sub-inspector Janes unrolled one and held it up, and informed

Aliens Restriction (Consolidation Order, 1914.

UNDER the provisions of the above Order, the COUNTY BOROUGH OF HASTINGS, as well as the whole County of Sussex, has now been declared a prohibited area, and all Aliens of whatever Nationality must therefore forthwith present themselves at the CENTRAL POLICE STATION, STATION ROAD, for the purpose of being registered, and at the same time produce documentary evidence of their Nationality, and a recent photograph about two inches square.

All alien enemies, viz. GERMANS, AUSTRIANS, and HUNGARIANS, must leave the town within four days from this date, unless they have a written authority of the Chief Constable to remain, and before leaving must obtain a permit to enable them to travel, and give notice of their intended destination.

Aliens failing to comply with the above Order will render themselves liable to a penalty of £100, or six months' imprisonment.

F. JAMES,
Chief Constable and Registration Officer.
Central Police Station,
Hastings.

November 2nd, 1914.

The notification placed in the *HSLO*, giving 'aliens' four days to leave town. It appeared on the front page, but hidden amongst so many prominent adverts for shops and entertainments.

them that a similar notification had been printed in the *HSLO* of 31st October. Somehow they had both missed it. Mrs Krebs assured him that, had they known about this new requirement, of course they would have complied, just as they had willingly registered with the police.

Because the four days' notice to leave had expired the day before, Sub-inspector Janes ordered the couple to accompany him immediately to the magistrates' court, where he placed them before the bench: ex-Madras Cavalry Captain Augustus Colville, Dr E.R. Mansell and Dr Kaye-Smith (father of Sheila, the future famous novelist). The couple were charged with contravening the Aliens Restriction Order by remaining in Hastings, 'a prohibited area for all alien enemies', after 6th November. Hearing herself described as an 'alien' and an 'enemy', Alice pointed out that she was from Croydon! She was then informed that she had 'become German' by marrying Hugo, despite never having even visited the country. Mr Krebs asked politely if they might apply for the special permit, but he was informed that it was 'too late'.

Capt Colville ordered them to pay a joint fine of £50 (the equivalent of £5,000 today). Luckily the couple had enough saved, because the alternative was to both go to prison for six months with hard labour! Mrs Krebs spoke up in protest, but Mr Krebs, depressed and beaten down by the war, just wanted to quickly pay the £50 without arguing. However, they would still have to leave town. They were given just four days to pack up and go.

When the devastated couple arrived back home at noon they were in state of total shock. Hugo was barely able to speak. They sat in their dining room and looked around at the lovely home they had created together, at their furniture and belongings and wondered how on earth they could move in just four days. On top of that, before they left town they had to obtain mugshots, exactly two inches square, apply for and receive a permit to travel from the police, and tell them the exact address to which they were moving. There was too much to organise in too such a time. And where would they go? What would happen to their home in their absence? For how long would they be banned from Hastings? Would the war be over by Christmas, as some pundits claimed? Or would it drag on for years? Could the British Government actually take their house? So many questions and no answers. They felt bewildered and panicky. Hugo said Alice could stay with her brother in London, but had no plan for himself. He went upstairs, returned with some newspapers and threw them onto a chair — perhaps he intended to search for the notice — then went back up to visit the bathroom.

Hugo was such a gentle, quiet man that when Alice heard the bathroom door slam shut loudly she immediately went upstairs. She could get the bathroom door open just enough to see Hugo collapsed on the floor, but he was blocking the door and she had not the strength to push him out of the way. She flew downstairs and out into the street, shouted to a passing boy to fetch Dr Farnfield, then ran the few dozen yards to the corner of Mount Road and entered Clive Vale Police Station. Sub-inspector Janes accompanied her back to the house, shouldered the bathroom door and found Mr Krebs doubled up on the floor. There was blood everywhere and a razor lay nearby. Moments later, Dr Farnfield arrived, but there was nothing he could do; Hugo had slashed his wrists and cut his throat and was dead.

At the inquest Borough Coroner William Glenister was at pains to absolve the police from legal or moral responsibility for the man's suicide. Krebs was 'an alien enemy', and as such should have left town on 6th. Notices had been issued. An application to remain may have been granted. The couple were liable to a fine of £200, but the magistrates had let them off with £50. The man must have lost his mental balance, clearly he was not in his right mind. That was the only possible conclusion, Mr Glenister said. His jury returned a verdict of 'Suicide whilst temporarily insane' and feigned sympathy for the widow.

Alice was left utterly devastated. She had lost the love of her life, an innocent, harmless man who had contributed hard work and taxes to this country for decades. Now she was made to suffer the pain and indignity of having him publicly labelled as insane in sixteen newspapers across the UK.

Prior to this incident the *HSLO* had published a number of news reports, articles, letters and editorial pieces that expressed blatant hostility to Germans who lived in England (see facing page). Mr Krebs must have seen at least some of them, and they surely must have hurt him deeply. Even as he lay bleeding in his bathroom that day's *HSLO* carried yet another vitriolic opinion-piece by the editor on the subject of the despised 'enemy aliens'.

Before the expulsion order was introduced, Hastings Police knew the addresses of all 'aliens' who had registered with them. The town had seven police stations, and so the bobbies knew all the locals. Instead of relying on posters or adverts, it is a pity that they did not visit the handful of aliens on their beats. The Krebses lived barely a minute from Clive Vale Police Station.

Once she was no longer the wife of an alien, but his widow, Alice was permitted to stay in Hastings, but without the man with whom she had spent nearly all her adult life. Hugo left her £1,700 (£167,000 today) so would never go without, but at just fifty-six she had many years of lonely widowhood ahead.

In 1924 she bought a three bedroom villa in Alfred Road, in which she kept an ever-growing menagerie of cats. One late night in 1937 as she crossed the road near her home she was hit by a motor car. As she lay in her hospital bed she admitted that she simply did not look before stepping into the road. She died from her injuries.

References: *HSLO* 24 and 31 October; 7 November 1914. The *HSLO* articles reproduced on the facing page have been edited to fit the space and to remove irrelevancies and repetitions whilst remaining strictly faithful to the meaning.

ROUNDING UP THE ENEMY IN OUR MIDST

(HSLO 24th October 1914)

In spite of evidence of daring espionage, the Home Office has been asking English people to believe that every German in their midst is the honest man and patriotic citizen which he pretends to be. Heavy pressure has been required to shake the confidence in our alien enemies' good intentions, but at last public opinion has prevailed, and the Home Office has issued an Order directing the Police to arrest all Germans 'of military age'. Information showing how this Order affects Hastings is given in another column. It is satisfactory to learn that the Authorities here have already carried out the Order with energy. Let us hope that the information they possessed of the whereabouts and pretensions of Germans in the town has enabled them to do the job thoroughly.

It is childish to talk about the injustice to certain aliens who have resided here for years. It may be that some innocent Germans...will be included in the round up, but it is better that this should happen than that any risk should be run of danger to England from the enemy.

It is the duty of every English man and woman to render the Police all possible assistance in its dealings with the enemy in our midst. Information of any value should never be withheld, even though it refers to somebody who has gained the confidence of his neighbours through his apparently good behaviour throughout a residence of several years.

SHOULD ALL ALIEN ENEMIES BE ROUNDED UP?

(HSLO 31st October 1914)

The Leading Article in last Saturday's issue of this paper favoured the rounding up of all Germans as the only way to completely deal with and overcome the spy danger. [A few] take the view that an order for the arrest of Germans is harsh and unfair. It could be that in some cases the Order inflicts punishment on innocent and inoffensive aliens, but the first consideration must be this country's welfare, and even though action that is necessary carries with it suffering for a few innocent aliens enjoying the hospitality of this country, it must be persisted in. We are at war with Germany and until this War is finished Germans in this country should be regarded as England's enemies, and each one should be assumed to be a potential spy. This is the sane and safe way to proceed; any other course leaves the door open for espionage, with possible disaster in its train. It may seem cruel to arrest aliens who have long resided with us and have always been looked upon as law abiding citizens, but it must be remembered that many cases of espionage have proceeded from this class of apparently harmless aliens, who have gained the confidence of their English neighbours. I notice that some people regard the proposal to round up all Germans as panicky advice. It is nothing of the kind: it is simply sound commonsense, a reasonable endeavour to prevent spies from playing their game.

GERMANS NATURALISED IN ENGLAND ARE STILL GERMAN SUBJECTS

Some people say there is no necessity to deal with Germans who have become naturalised Englishmen. They seem to be labouring under the delusion that they cannot damage England because they are no longer German subjects. This is a mistake. Every German is a German subject so long as he has not renounced his German nationality. Every German who has acquired British nationality is therefore liable to all the obligations of German nationality...including such duties as serving in the German Army, if he returns to Germany, and rendering that Army all possible assistance by sending useful information if he remains in England — commonly called spying.

13 to 8 Pelham Crescent prior to 1921 and (below) today. Clearly the chimney stack between nos. 10 and 11 was rebuilt.

1921

SAFELY TUCKED UP IN BED

PELHAM CRESCENT

In the 1920s it was neither naff nor embarrassing for a teenage East End boy to go on holiday with his sister and her mates, and so John Smith was happy to accompany Kate for a week in Hastings. He was eighteen and the girls were two years older. They booked two rooms in Aston House, a grand building within a stately Georgian crescent, facing the seafront and near all the attractions.

The house was owned by sixty-four-year-old Carlotta Buckland, a well known and highly respected widow, who ran it as a boarding house for thirty-eight years. It was left to her by her late husband, who had inherited it from his uncle, George Norman, paymaster-in-chief of the Royal Navy. Widowed in 1906, she remarried in 1907 and lost her second husband in 1914. She then engaged a young Londoner, Adelaide Tucker, to co-manage the house, and their happy partnership lasted twenty years.

On the morning of Saturday 10th September, after saying farewell to their parents and younger siblings, John and Kate met up with her friends and travelled to Hastings. The larger of the rooms had a balcony and a sea view, so the girls quickly bagged that: Kate and Doreen Hart would share the double bed, whilst Kate Pescud had the single all to herself. John took the top floor rear room, next to a pair of funloving young ladies from Birmingham who were sharing a double-bedded room at the front. After two wonderful days of seaside fun and laughter, the group turned in at about ten o' clock on the Sunday night, looking forward eagerly to five more days of sightseeing and amusement, and blissfully unaware that within hours one of them would be dead.

'Whilst the people of Hastings lay in their beds listening to the wild, mad buffeting of the violent gale which broke over the town', wrote a reporter in the HSLO, 'a tragedy, swift and terrible, was occurring in their midst.' The wind swept along at a tremendous pace and came hard up against a chimney stack which lay across the dividing wall between 10 and 11 Pelham Crescent. The stack was massive because it was built to serve both houses — a total of eighteen flues. It was 12ft high and 30ft long and held a row of eighteen square pots made of cement. The weight of the stack was estimated at nine tons.

At about 3.25am a particularly ferocious gust blew the entire stack over sideways, sending it crashing through the slate roof of no.10 and into its loft, splintering the heavy timber rafters and shattering into large, heavy, jagged chunks of brick and cement. The sheer weight of this wreckage caused the loft floor to give way and the two Brummies sharing a bed in the top floor front room were showered with bits of chimney stack, pots, roof tiles and rafters. Their room's floorboards cracked under the strain and their iron bedstead — with them still in it — descended through the floor and into the room below, along with some hefty wooden furniture. Seeing their ceiling bulge, crack and split, Kate and her pals sprung out of their beds and crouched in a corner, arms instinctively protecting their heads. Seconds later the ceiling was ripped apart and it felt like the entire building was crashing down on them. Huge planks of splintered floorboards, chunks of lath and plaster, lumps of brickwork, a wardrobe, a chest, a dressing table and an iron bedstead — containing two screaming women — crashed down into the room. When everything settled the three girls unshielded their eyes and looked around. The scene was one of diabolical ruin. Their first priority was to rescue the sobbing girls who had been plummeted into their room. One of them, though badly bruised, was able to get herself out and walk, but the other had received severe injuries to her back, and had to await ambulance assistance.

House manager Adelaide Tucker, who slept in the front room of the basement, was awakened by bits of chimney falling into the area outside her window. Going up to the ground floor in her dressing gown she found frightened guests collecting on the stairs. She sent at once for the police.

Every available officer was despatched to the crescent, with sergeants Bush and Tapp taking charge of the evacuation. Thomas Chessum, chief of Hastings Fire Brigade, was summoned by telephone. When he arrived Adelaide told him that both top rooms were occupied, so he immediately made his way up the several flights of stairs. The front room was nearly empty, everything having disappeared into the room below. The door to the top rear bedroom would not open, so a hatchet was brought up to smash in the door panels. Looking through the ragged hole Chessum saw that a large heap of debris prevented him from opening the door. No.2 Section of the Fire Brigade forced the door and managed to push away just enough of the wreckage to gain entry.

The scene was one of utter chaos: bricks, roof slates, lathes, plaster and rafters lay strewn about. Through the thick, dust-laden air they discerned a bedstead, but no sign of a guest. Then they found a second bed, bent and twisted under heaps of assorted bits of smashed-up building and began to remove the rubble, not knowing what lay beneath. Eventually they found a teenage boy, laying on his right side with his eyes closed, the bedclothes pulled up to his ears. He did not move or respond to them. Dr Francis Daunt, who was at the scene, was brought in to attend to him, but he pronounced life extinct.

Both rooms on the floor beneath were in a state of wild confusion. The ceilings had ragged gaps, revealing splintered beams and ancient rafters with bent nails protruding at wild angles. Lath and plaster had fallen everywhere, and everything was covered with a thick coating of century-old dust. The ceilings in several other rooms had also collapsed.

There had been forty-one persons sleeping in the house at the time of the accident, and so it was a miracle that there was only one fatality, one person hospitalised and four slightly injured. Over the next few days a number of guests related their personal anecdotes of being caught up in the drama, describing in vivid detail the terrifying experience they had endured.

The inquest on John Henry Smith was held on Wednesday 14th September at All Saints' Girls' School by Borough Coroner W. J. Glenister. Dr Daunt said the deceased had sustained considerable bruising of the head, neck and trunk from debris falling on him during sleep, but the cause of death was asphyxiation. The coroner remarked that the 'exceedingly sad and pathetic aspect of the case' was that the poor boy had been 'looking forward joyfully to spending a happy holiday', without 'the slightest idea of what was going to happen.' John was a smart lad who had already embarked on a career as a clerk in a marine insurance company. The coroner referred to the the accident as a 'crushing blow' to the Smith family, to whom he extended his heartfelt sympathy. Breaking with the usual custom of attributing the accident to an 'act of God', he blamed instead an act of 'natural force'.

The jury returned a verdict of 'accidental death'. Mr Smith expressed thanks to the coroner for his courtesy and consideration, and took his son's body home to Leytonstone for interment.

The accident could not have been foreseen. The stack had withstood high, even gale force winds, scores of times over its hundred-year existence and had never budged. A builder had repaired it just three years previously and saw it was in good order. The borough surveyor explained that, because the stack sat at right-angles to the face of the cliff, during high winds the back of the house and the cliff formed a channel, causing the wind to strike the stack 'broadside-on', which inflicted a heavy strain upon it. There were no supports, so it would receive the full force and be subjected to a pressure equal to five tons.

The damage to the house was estimated at £500 (£22,000 today). On enquiry it emerged that the incident, deemed an 'act of God', was not covered by insurance, and Carlotta Buckland did not have the means to pay. What is more, she was facing the loss of her entire income during the period of reconstruction. Councillor Meads suggested the town assist her by donating to a repair fund, for which an account was opened the London County Westminster Bank.

Although the *HSLO* did not report how much was raised, the boarding house reopened a year later and thrived once again under the women's joint management. When Carlotta died in 1934 the press referred to Adelaide as her 'constant companion'. Adelaide married soon afterwards and emigrated to Canada, where she died in 1977.

References: *HSLO* 17 September & 19 November 1921; *Sheffield Independent* 13 September 1921.

In August 1928 this beautiful motorcycle combination was acquired by Hastings Police. The Nineham case was one of the first times it was used. Unfortunately we do not know the names of the officers lined up in a corner of Priory Meadow for this commemorative photo-shoot on 15th September. Perhaps one of the men in civvies is Sub-inspector Small.

MURDER AND MADNESS

MOUNT PLEASANT ROAD

At the age of sixty-seven Gertie Nineham led a quiet, contented life. She and her only surviving child, a son, shared a five-roomed terraced house on Mount Pleasant Road. George was thirty-eight and since leaving school had worked for solicitors Young, Coles & Langdon at 1 Bank Buildings, rising to the trusted position of cost clerk and bookkeeper. He had never left his employer nor his mother, except between 1915 and 1919 when he served as a gunner in the Royal Field Artillery in Bombay, Lahore, Basrah and Mesopotamia, where he caught malaria. He was a fair-haired, smooth-shaven, pleasant-looking fellow of slender build. According to his army records, at age twenty-six he stood 5ft 6½ in his socks and had a thirty-three-and-a-half inch chest.

Gertie, born Gertrude Alice Moyes in 1861, grew up at 22 Gensing Road and 16 Devonshire Road. Her father was a carpenter and her mother was a lodging house keeper. She married tailor James Nineham in 1887 and within three years they had two sons, one of whom died in infancy. James died in 1903, when George was fourteen, and since then it had been just the two of them. They were, by all accounts, devoted to one another.

George had only one close friend: William Ennis, shop manager for J. Hepworth & Son, a gentlemen's outfitters at 35 Queen's Road. They had been acquainted for eighteen years, close friends for three, and met nearly every day, often more than once. Each morning William would leave his flat at 63 Beaconsfield Road and go along Hughenden Road to Mount Pleasant Road, where George was always waiting for him. They would walk together to central Hastings, where their workplaces were a hundred yards apart, and then met after work, sometimes lingering for a pint or two before walking home. William described George as 'a quiet, inoffensive man' who lived on terms of the greatest affection with his dear mother. He was a calm, reliable, dependable chap who led a dull, predictable, routine life.

On Saturday 27th October the friends met at 9pm for a drink in a pub in Queen's Road then ambled home together. They would meet in the morning at 9.30 after William visited a workmate's allotment. George did not turn up, and William saw a delivered milk bottle was still on the Ninehams' doorstep. Despite banging on the door and calling, he got no response and so hurried to a telephone box and called the police.

Sub-inspector Small climbed into the side-car of the shiny new police motorcycle combination and was driven swiftly to the house by P.C. Eldridge.

	1.	2.	3.	4.
1	Gertrude Alice Nineham	Head		50
2	George Alfred James Nineham	Son	22	

Law Clerk	429	Solicitors	428 Mother	—	Sussex S. Leonards-on-Sea Sussex Hastings

Signature _Gertrude Alice Nineham_

Postal Address _214 Priory Road, West Hill Hastings_

Details from the 1911 census. George completed it in his neat, clear, regular handwriting, then, as Head of Household, his mother signed it.

George's signature when he was twenty-six, taken from his army recruitment papers.

I am willing to fulfil the engagements made.

G. A. J. Nineham _____ SIGNATURE OF RECRUIT.

They walked through a neighbour's house to gain entry to the back yards then forced an entry into the scullery where they found George, in his pyjamas, draped over the cooker. He must have knelt down and gassed himself by putting his head in the oven and opening the gas tap without lighting it, thereby breathing in the noxious fumes. He then straightened up and, staying on his knees, passed out with his head resting on the gas hob. S.I. Small, who had been drilled in first aid, saved George's life by performing artificial respiration until Dr Channock Smith arrived. The casualty was conveyed to the Royal East Sussex Hospital in Cambridge Road in a St John Motor Ambulance. Later that night he regained consciousness and was expected to make a full recovery.

After he was removed the police searched the house. Upstairs, in the back bedroom, lying across her bed, and wearing her nightdress, was the battered, mutilated corpse of Gertie Nineham. A broken, bloodstained axe and an open cut-throat razor lay discarded on the carpet nearby.

The police surgeon Adolphus T. Field arrived at 2.30pm. This had clearly been a most ferocious attack on a defenceless old lady. Multiple head wounds had been inflicted by the axe, and there were also slash wounds on her neck and hand from the razor. Clearly she had put up her hand to shield herself from attack. She had been dead for about six or eight hours, placing the time of the attack at around 7am. The post mortem showed that she died of injuries to the brain and a haemorrhage caused by the gash in her throat.

Meanwhile at the RESH, P.C. Bertie Breach had been ordered to sit at George's bedside, in plain clothes for discretion. At one point George turned to him and enquired: 'Could you arrest anyone for murder?' Bertie said he could, and George continued: 'I have done one: I have murdered my mother'. Bertie asked if he realised what he was saying, then cautioned him.

The inquest, under coroner W.J. Glenister, was opened at the Market Hall in George Street on Tuesday 30th October. The police had tracked down the Ninehams' only living relative: Gertie's husband's brother, William. He had not seen them since attending his brother's funeral twenty-five years previously, but was asked to identify Gertie from memory. The inquest was then adjourned until 22nd January.[1] Gertie was interred the next day at the Borough Cemetery. There were two mourners: George's friend William and Gertie's brother-in-law.

On 31st October D.I. Milton interviewed George and took down his verbal statement: 'I do hereby declare that on the night of Saturday I did in a moment of madness kill my mother. I make this statement of my own free will; after being cautioned, I have read it over and it is true.'

George was questioned for two hours by Dr Frederick Ryott Taylor, the medical superintendent at Hellingly Asylum. He discovered that George 'had not associated with his fellows at school much, nor joined in games'. What is more, he had 'no inclination for marriage'. He had contemplated suicide and

---

1. It seems never to have been resumed.

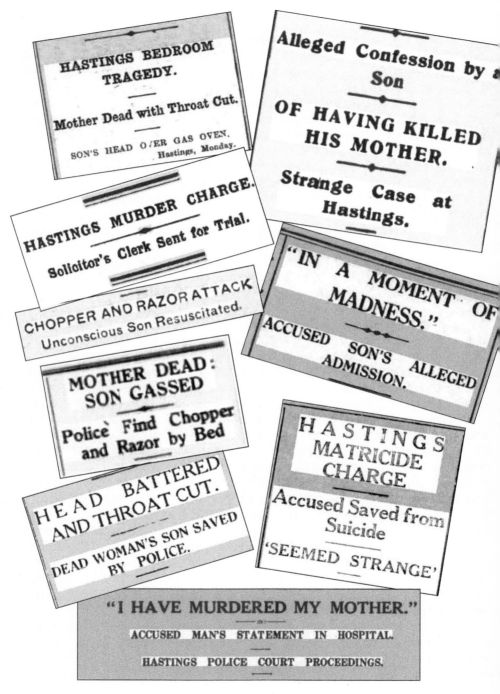

Some of the many headlines about the case published in newspapers across the UK.

also had 'feelings that he must harm someone'. 'Voices in his head' told him to kill Gertie.

It was not until 7th November that George was well enough to leave hospital. On that day, Sub-inspector Small and Detective Inspector Milton appeared at his bedside at 10.30am and informed him that he was to accompany them to the Central Police Station inide the town hall immediately. He was formally charged then taken into the adjacent courtroom for his initial hearing. Being still quite weak he was supported into the dock by a policeman and a gaoler. Standing in silence, his eyes downcast, he was remanded for a week.

On 14th November 'a crowd of morbid spectators' had gathered around the town hall to catch a glimpse of the evil mother-killer. George had fully recovered his health, and he sat still and silent in the lobby with his solicitor F.W. Morgan until his name was called. He then 'walked briskly into the Council Chamber,[2] and without hesitation or guidance took up his place...His former pallor had vanished. His face was slightly flushed and there was a bright, alert look in his eyes'. Alderman Hocking conducted the short but formal procedure. The public seats were chock-full and the eager gawpers obtained a good, long hard look at him, but ultimately it was an anticlimax: no evidence was taken and it was all over in minutes. George was simply remanded for another week.

At the third hearing, on 21st November, Mr Ross Pilcher Pashley of the CPS prosecuted and F.W. Morgan defended. The police court was 'crowded, every available seat being filled'. George 'stepped firmly into the dock...neatly dressed in a navy blue suit'. He was charged not only with murder but also with attempting to commit suicide (a criminal offence until 1961). The magistrates kindly allowed him to sit and he 'remained in a graven attitude, staring intently before him throughout the proceedings. The bloodstained axe and razor lay on the exhibits table. His attitude was one of utmost detachment, even when the gruesome finds in the house of tragedy were described in detail'.

Dr Taylor was called for the defence. George said that a voice he heard in the middle of the night told him to kill his mother. So he went downstairs, fetched the axe and did the deed. He thought she died from the first blow, but he continued the onslaught anyway. He had no recollection of using a razor. Taylor said George was 'not mentally normal'; he had 'acted under a morbid impulse which he could not resist', brought about by the 'auditory hallucinations'. He felt that George knew 'the nature and quality of the act he was doing', but 'did not appreciate its wickedness'. The killing appeared to be 'quite unpremeditated'; and his subsequent suicide attempt suggested insanity.

William Ennis also appeared for the defence. He backed up Dr Taylor: George had been acting rather queer for about a week before the incident. He 'did not reply intelligently to any remark I made' and sometimes 'looked dazed and vacant' with 'his eyes turned upwards'. On the evening of 27th October they

2. The courtroom was already occupied, so the hearing was instead conducted in the chamber.

had browsed a London evening paper together. Inside was a report about police breaking into a shop in Bath, where they found a newlywed dead on her bed, her head battered in. William's wife had known George since childhood. She said he was 'very quiet, very gentle, and a very nice fellow'. Of late he had not been sleeping well, and had been bothered by strange feelings and thoughts. Thinking he 'had a breakdown coming on', she bought him some Phospherine tablets (which contained valerian).

Mr Edwards, managing clerk at Young, Coles & Langdon, had known George for many years. He was 'on very affectionate terms with his mother' and 'always referred to her in a very nice way'. When he teased George about being single, he replied that he could never marry whilst his mother was alive. George had been behaving rather strangely of late, and sometimes poured a bucket of water over his head. At other times he looked vacant and would reply 'Eh?' to everything said to him.

The police officers and doctors gave evidence for the prosecution and George's written confession was read out. He was placed on a charge of 'wilful murder' and of 'attempting to commit suicide by inhaling coal gas', and was committed to stand trial at the next assizes.

In the meantime, Gertrude's will was examined. She had left everything she had, amounting to £284 15s 9d (about £17,000 today) to her son.

Although only two days earlier a Bill had been proposed in the House of Commons to abolish it, the death penalty was still in place in 1928. That year, in the UK, twenty-two people had already been hanged and two more were waiting on 'Death Row'. This was the fate that awaited George.

The Sussex Assizes opened on Friday 7th December. The first witness was Dr Watson, senior medical officer at Brixton Prison, who had kept George under observation' since 7th November. He was convinced that George was suffering from 'a mental disease'. Lately, his condition had become 'much worse'. Based on his opinion the jury concluded that George was 'insane and unfit to plead'. Mr Justice Rowlatt ordered him to be 'detained during His Majesty's pleasure'. He was sent to a lunatic asylum.

By curious happenstance, when the *Daily Herald* covered the Nineham story, the report that followed was an update on the Bath murder which George had read about just hours before he killed Gertie. It transpired that her husband had been charged. By further coincidence, in February 1929 he, too, would be found guilty but insane and, just like George, confined in a lunatic asylum.

The document on the facing page reveals that, in May 1937, after less than nine years in an asylum, George was released. In 1939 he was recorded in lodgings in Lymington, Hampshire; he gave his occupation as 'solicitor's clerk'.

The next public record relating to George is his marriage on 14th October 1946. At fifty-eight Daisy Montague was a year his senior and had a remarkable back story. On her sixteenth birthday she had married a mechanical dentist twice her age, by whom she was seven months pregnant. They had four children

The document above was written from an address in Knightsbridge in July 1939. It is a declaration from George to the War Office explaining why he had no discharge papers relating to his service in WWI. It reads: 'In November 1928, at Hastings, Sussex, I had a severe mental breakdown, and became an inmate of a mental institution until May 1937, during which time my home was sold up and I presume all my private papers were destroyed at that time.'

and then split up. They never divorced, and so it was only after her husband died in 1946 that she was able to marry George. Whether she knew he was a real-life axe-murderer, who can say? Daisy died in 1963 and George in 1965. He must have had another breakdown, for he died in Kent County Mental Hospital at Chartham, aged seventy-six.

The prequel

This extraordinary tale has a tragic prequel. When George was a teenager his parents were in their early forties and had enjoyed fifteen years of wedded happiness. Doubtless they expected to grow old together. James, a tailor, kept himself fit by taking long walks in the country or town, sometimes accompanied by Gertie and George.

On Tuesday 25th August 1903 James set out to walk to his barber for a haircut whilst Gertie prepared lunch for them all. They planned to spend the afternoon taking a leisurely stroll in the sunshine together; however, James failed to return as arranged. He never saw his home again.

About 12.30pm Olive Thurger, the wife of a signalman, looked out from her home at 12 Hurrell Road and saw a man on the Broomgrove railway bridge. She watched as he ran eastwards down the embankment and onto the track, climbing over a 3ft high fence on the way. A steam engine and its train of empty carriages were making a shunt movement over to the other line to change direction.[3] The fireman spotted a man lying on the track and climbed down. He was faced with a ghastly sight. His train had run over the man's leg and sliced it off beneath the knee. He fetched the first aid box and he and the driver used some bandages as a torniquet. With the help of the guard and a train examiner from Ore sheds they lifted the man into the brakevan. They took his name and address and handed it to the station master, then set out for Hastings, where the station staff took James to the East Sussex Hospital at White Rock.

The station master at Ore called on Gertie and, sparing her the ghastly truth, pretended that James had only 'broken his leg' in an accident. She rushed to the hospital but was told he was too poorly to see her. James's left leg must have been run over by two carriage wheels, because from the knee down it had been sliced into three pieces. The surgeon saved what he could, tidied up the wound, stitched it and bound it up with copious bandages. Gertie was finally allowed to see him at 8pm. Although conscious he was too ill to converse. She returned every day for three days, but each time they turned her away.

On Friday 28th August the house surgeon amputated the remainder of James's leg, right up to the hip joint, to save his life. The following day, because they feared he was going to die, they allowed Gertie stay by his side as he drifted in and out of consciousness from the strong drugs they had administered to help with the awful pain. He 'rambled somewhat of engines and trains', and told her that his suicidal action was 'the work of a moment'. That night he died. The cause was blood poisoning.

The inquest was held by W.J. Glenister, the same man who would enquire into Gertie's death twenty-five years later. Gertie explained that James had been ill for three weeks with dyspepsia (indigestion). Although he suffered from bouts of depression he had never once spoken of suicide. The house surgeon who conducted the post mortem said that, whilst under his care, James suffered from delusions and his speech was incoherent, which suggested that he suffered from 'melancholic mania'. The coroner's jury returned a verdict of 'accidental death'.

References: *HSLO* 29 August & 5 September 1903; 3, 10, 17 & 24 November and 8 December 1928. *Daily Herald* 29 October 1928.

---

3. Trains still make this shunt movement today, and the author had the great pleasure of playing her part in it periodically over a period of five years.

1929

Canine despair

Grand Parade

On the evening of Tuesday 16th July holidaymakers strolling along the promenade near the foot of London Road were astonished to see a large, unaccompanied retriever walk down the beach and along a groyne, then plunge into the sea and swim straight out towards HMS *Centaur,* then anchored in deep water.

Captain George Vernon Conquest Blake, son of the editor of the *Sporting Life*, was the proprietor of the Grosvenor Hotel at 21 Grand Parade. From his balcony he watched the dog through his field glasses until it became a tiny speck in the distance. Realising the animal needed to be rescued, he summoned Captain Slade, a guest at the hotel, and together they rushed out and launched a rowing boat.

By then an ever-increasing crowd had collected on the promenade and beach; all eyes scanned the horizon, hoping to see the dog paddle back towards the shore. They watched the two captains row as hard and as fast as they could for a distance of half a mile. But the dog had completely disappeared; it had become exhausted and drowned.

When the rowing boat returned to the shore, Captain Blake was met by a very distressed married couple, who explained that they had recently moved from a house at Silverhill, that had a large garden, in which their dog loved to frolic, to a gardenless flat at Warrior Square. Ever since they arrived in their new home the dog had been restless, pining and depressed. Somehow it slipped out unnoticed, determined to put an end to its existence.

'At first I thought the dog was taking a swim because of the heat,' said Captain Blake, 'but when I learned the facts I came to the conclusion that it was a deliberate case of suicide.'

SATURDAY, JULY 20, 1929.

DOG COMMITS SUICIDE.
:o:

LARGE CROWDS WATCH THRILLING RESCUE EFFORT.

PLUNGE OFF ST. LEONARDS GROYNE.

Sergeant N. Read (centre) and two other non-commissioned officers of 'H' Company of the 5th Cinque Ports Battalion of the Royal Sussex Regiment. This unit of the Territorial Force had its HQ at the Drill Hall at Grove Road (now Hi-Tec timber, the rear of which can be seen looming over Aldi's car park). Nelson joined soon after it was formed on 1st April 1908 and for the following six years was kept busy with a non-stop round of meetings, drills, marches, training sessions, shooting competitions, and yearly summer camps.

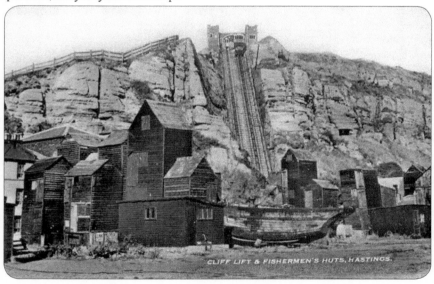

CLIFF LIFT & FISHERMEN'S HUTS, HASTINGS.

The East Hill Lift was, upon completion, Britain's steepest funicular railway, a title it lost in 1910, regained in 1991, and still holds. (Steeper ones existed at Broadstairs between 1910 and 1991 and Margate between 1913 and 1978.) The cars in use today are sadly not the mahogany-framed originals, which were replaced in 1973, at the same time as the lift was converted from hydraulic to electric operation.

The Funicular Mystery

Rock-a-Nore Road

Nelson 'Nel' Read was a very ordinary man. Born in Ore on 31st August 1881, the son of an unskilled labourer, his elementary education set him on the same path. His childhood home was North Row, a long terrace of workers' cottages now known as Winchelsea Road, and, as a typical working class lad would, he loved football, and played for St Helen's and St Clement's Rovers, where he was an average performer.

In 1902 he married a woman with a laundry business, which she carried on after marriage, employing her sister and niece, who also lived with them. The Reads were conventional, respectable, hard working and wholly unremarkable, and they produced two children, one of each sex, spaced nicely apart.

The most interesting thing Nel did in his life, apart from dying prematurely and in a mysterious manner, was to serve for fourteen years in the territorials, rising to sergeant.

When the First World War began in August 1914, his battalion was mobilised immediately under the command of local solicitor Lieutenant Colonel F.G. Langham VD.[1] Its first job was to go to Dover, where after a day manning road blocks they had to sleep on the cold stone floor of the castle. After a spell at the Tower of London they proceeded to France on SS *Pancras*, landing at Boulogne on 18th February 1915. The battalion was assigned to other brigades and divisions, and took part in the battles of Aubers Ridge, the Somme, Ypres, Piave, Asiago Plateau, Vittorio Veneto and Val d'Assa.

Nel spent nearly four years on some of the most infamously bloody battlefields, and yet somehow he came out alive. His youngest brother Arthur was not so lucky. The young husband and new dad joined up on in March 1915 as a gunner in the Royal Field Artillery and was killed on the fields of Ypres in August 1916.[2]

After the war Nel began to work for Hastings Corporation as a labourer on the roads, eventually rising to foreman. He and his family moved into 88 Victoria Avenue, Ore, on the corner of Clifton Road. In 1928, aged forty-six, he started a new job working at the East Hill Lift, and within two years was promoted to chief attendant.

---

1. Frederick George, one of several legal Langhams who feature in both volumes of *Strange Exits*.
2. His wife, who lived at 20 Scrivens Buildings in Crown Lane, was granted a war pension of 18s 6d a week whilst her children were dependent.

The idea to build a cliff railway was prompted by the opening of the West Hill Lift in 1891. That had been a private enterprise, but the East Hill equivalent was built by the corporation. One eulogy in its favour read:

There are multitudes of people whom the apex of the East Hill, the glorious country which lies on a level with its summit and the valley spreading northward and eastward, are, to speak without irreverence, almost what the Promised Land was to Moses. They look upon the fair, faraway region, and they long for it, but it is wholly inaccessible to them. And may I not also say that there are many well-to-do residents, people with weak chests, to whom new pleasure of life would be given were they able, without physical effort, to scale the great hill, and feast their eyes on the grand scenery, and drink the ozone of the local Alps.

The cutting, which at its deepest is over 120ft, would carry the 22ft wide track at an incline of 1 in 1.28 for 267ft. It was originally worked by water balance, each tower housing an iron tank containing 1,200 gallons. At the foot of the tracks a tank held the discharged water and returned it to the top of the hill.

Construction began on 1st March 1901. As the cliff face was excavated, a skull was found (and shattered by a workman's pick-axe!) followed by a fragment of ancient wall and a trench full of old bones. The upper station was intended to resemble a castle, hence the castellated roofline. (Over the years many a local has chuckled at naive visitors mistaking it for Hastings Castle.) It had a waiting room, a refreshment room and public toilets. The lower station, styled like a chapel, was the final part to be completed, and the lift was ready to 'carry many hundreds onto the summit of the beautiful grassy plateau which overlooks the blue waters of the English Channel.'

On Saturday 9th August 1902, the day of the deferred coronation of Edward VII and Queen Alexandra, the council unveiled its new tourist attraction and amenity. Six hundred passengers were carried, before the mechanism suffered a breakdown, leaving hundreds more disappointed.

The lift was a big hit with visitors and locals. 'Everybody speaks very highly of the elegant cars...and the convenience and comfort in general.' It came at a price, though: the hill had been disfigured. 'No good can come', wrote the editor of the *HSLO*, 'from indulging in lachrymose lamentations over the fact that the beauty of the hill has to some extent been sacrificed.'

The corporation hoped to recoup the building costs of £6,000 from ticket sales. For religious reasons it did not run on Sundays (nor did the town's trams), which reduced the takings. When Sunday working began in 1904 receipts rose, and were published weekly. It continued to be profitable for decades: for example, it was reported in 1929 that, whilst the White Rock Pavilion showed a loss of £3,000, the East Hill lift made a profit of £244.

On Monday morning, 15th September 1930, lift attendant Joe Emerson arrived at work at 8.30am. He found the outer iron gates unlocked, and assumed that his guv'nor, Nelson, had arrived before him, though he was not due in till 9.15. Nel's duty was to man the lower station, but he was nowhere to be seen. The doors to the cars and track were locked, so Joe checked the pump-room and looked up the line, to no avail. Harry Morton,[3] the engineer, arrived at 9am, went to the upper station by the steps, and did not see Nelson.

The left hand car was standing at the foot of the incline, and at 9.25am Joe sent it on its preliminary ascent. 'As it moved away I noticed something in the water in the tank over which it had been standing. I looked again and saw it was the top of a man's head. The water was only about 4ft deep.' He telephoned Harry Morton at the upper station, and together they raised the body above the water enough to see that it was Nelson, and that he was dead. With assistance from P.C. Collins they recovered the body.

Nel had climbed into the tank many times, but never when alone, and only when it was nearly empty, in order to clear the suction pipe in the sump hole. Both Joe and Harry were puzzled: there was no need for Nel to have entered the tank that day and, besides, it was a two-man job which he always carried out with Harry. It was possible, though difficult, to get into the tank from the pump-room, but easier to enter it from the side of the car. The body was found at the extreme left of the tank, right underneath the spot where the car was standing. Although Nel's jacket was off and his shirt sleeves were rolled up as though ready for some manual work, he was wearing his ordinary boots and not the rubber Wellingtons which he always donned before entering the tank.

P.C. Collins applied artificial respiration until Dr Daunt arrived and told him that his efforts were redundant: Nel had been dead for about an hour. The post mortem confirmed the cause as asphyxia from drowning.

At the inquest, held at the Market Hall in George Street, Nel's wife Mary Annie was so distressed that she was allowed to go home immediately after giving her brief deposition. On Monday Nel rose at 6am, did some work in the garden, and over breakfast at 7am mentioned having to do something to the suction pipe on the lift. He left home just after 7.30.

Having remarked that a conscious person cannot accidentally drown in water that only reached to his chest, the coroner concluded that Nelson must have had some kind of fainting attack, which would not show up on a post mortem, then fallen into the tank and drowned whilst passed out. An open verdict was recorded, the coroner expressing sympathy with the widow and family.

References: *HSLO* 16 August 1902; 20 September 1930. *Portsmouth Evening News* 17 September 1930. www.ww1rollofhonour.co.uk

3. Harry was the brother of Joseph Morton, stepfather of John Payne, the subject of the next chapter, 'The Plank'.

Artist's impression of the lorry falling into the sea. It seems that the artist did not visit the scene, as the lorry does not match the one in the photograph above. *Illustrated Police News* 19 May 1932.

Above right: photograph of the tipper lorry after it had been righted at low tide. *Below left:* the top of the wall where the truck went over (photographed after the railing was restored) and (*below*) the wall and ledge looking south at low tide. *HSLO.*

1932

The Plank

Rock-a-Nore Road

At 3.15pm on 10th May John Payne,[1] an employee of Hastings Corporation, drove a lorry-load of rubble in a 30 cwt[2] tipper truck to the corporation tip at the extreme eastern end of Rock-a-Nore to dump it into the sea. To facilitate this, the tip attendant had removed a section of railing, but to stop drivers from backing over the edge, he laid a long plank of wood across the gap, resting it against two upright posts.

John reversed the lorry until the rear tyres touched the plank. He wound up the tipper and most of the rubble slid out. To dislodge the remainder he shunted the lorry forwards and backwards, bumping it against the plank. On the third attempt the plank fell flat and the wheels rolled off the edge of the wall. The lorry might have been grounded on its chassis, but the weight of the tipper being upright pulled it backwards. The lorry turned a half-somersault as it plummeted thirty feet and plunged into the sea. It was high tide, so the vehicle was submerged in 15ft of water, and John was trapped inside the upturned cab.

Witnesses shouted frantically for help, a lifebelt was thrown in and two fishing boats, the *Kathleen* and the *Albatross*, were launched. The dangerous currents and masses of debris made the rescuers' task extremely hazardous. At great personal risk lifeboat-man Johnnie Hart climbed from a boat onto the lorry to the cheers of onlookers and secured ropes to it, which he threw up to the crowd of spectators which included John's stepfather, Joe Morton. They tried their best but could not raise the cab high enough to save John's life, and he drowned trapped in his cab. As the tide ebbed Hart did eventually manage to release the body and haul it into a boat.

Coroner Harry Davenport Jones asked some pertinent questions about the corporation's dodgy practices. There had once been a substantial safety buffer, which was bolted firmly to the posts, but they had taken it away. It was the attendant's bright idea to use a plank to prevent vehicles from reversing over the edge. Returning a verdict of 'death by misadventure', the jury said that the corporation must take steps to increase safety at the tip.

John was interred in the Borough Cemetery. Forty-one and single, he lived with his mother and stepfather, a haulage contractor who owned the tipper lorry and hired it to Hastings Corporation. The corporation refused to pay compensation to the family but offered to cover the funeral costs.

References: *HSLO* 14 & 21 May 1932.

1. Joe's brother Harry makes a cameo appearance in 'The Funicular Mystery'.
2. cwt = a hundredweight, the equivalent to fifty kilos.

JOKE ENDS IN DEATH

Boy Found Hanging in Shop

1902 TRAGEDY RECALLED

In 1902 there was a hanging tragedy at 37, George-street, Hastings, which is now occupied by Mr. H. A. Boyd, photographer, and on Saturday afternoon an assistant at the shop, Frank Charles Jerry Smale, aged 15 years and nine months, of 119, Sembrook-road, Hastings, was found hanging on the first floor from a rope leading from the left. He died the following day.

Photo: Boyd, Hastings

Clipping from the *HSLO*, 27 November 1937. By coincidence, Gifford had taken a photo of Frank just two days before and so was able to supply one to the newspaper.

36–37 George Street today.

THE JOKER

GEORGE STREET

Frank Charles Jerry Smale was a lucky boy: as soon as he turned fourteen he landed a dream job working as an assistant to a photographer. His dad was only a labourer and had no trade to teach him, and Mr H.A. Boyd was giving him the opportunity to train for a profession. He'd be working in a shop at 37 George Street alongside the boss's teenage son, Harry Gifford Leonard Boyd, known simply as Gifford.

Frank was an exceedingly cheerful lad, a practical joker and amateur comedian, and the shop offered him great potential for some brilliant pranks. An opportunity presented itself when he genuinely slipped and fell down some stairs. As he hit the floor he decided not to get up but to lie still and play dead, in order to frighten Gifford, just for a lark. It worked a treat, scared the living daylights out of him! Frank cracked up laughing at Gifford for falling for it. The four-and-a-half-year age gap really showed: Gifford was by then a young man of twenty embarking on a serious profession; he found Frank's so-called 'jokes' rather childish and not remotely amusing.

Local rumour had it that in 1902 a man had hanged himself in that very shop. Frank, who clearly had a taste for the macabre, derived great satisfaction from relating this chilling tale to anyone who would listen, including his mother, and watching them squirm.

On Saturday 20th November Frank asked his mother to press a clean shirt for him as he would be going out on the town that evening. At work in the afternoon he chopped up some wood for the stove and as he swept up Gifford told him he was popping out and would not be long. Frank realised it was the perfect time to pull his Best Prank Ever. It was all planned and he had waited for the opportunity to put into practice. Gifford would get the shock of his life; he would be totally spooked out, and it would provide a hilarious and entertaining tale with which to regale his mates later on.

When Gifford returned at about 4.30 he called out to Frank but received no reply. Wanting the boy to make a pot of tea, he went through to the back room to seek him out. Something above his head caught his attention and he looked up to see Frank larking about again: this time he was pretending to be 'The Hanged Man' from the story he had been going on about.

Frank had mocked up the gruesome suicide by tying a washing line to a staple in the roof beams of the loft. There was a trap door in the first storey floor and he planned to create maximum horror by having his feet dangling

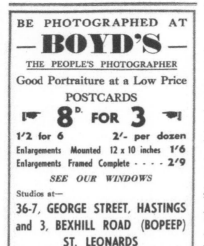
through it, so when Gifford returned they would initially be the only thing he saw.

Gifford sighed when he saw Frank's tasteless joke, but as his gaze lingered on his workmate he realised that he was not supporting himself in any way: he really was hanging by his neck. He flew up the stairs and, whilst supporting Frank's weight with one hand, cut the washing line just above the noose with the other. He laid him on the floor and discovered to his immense relief that he was still breathing. The silly prank had somehow gone horribly wrong. Thank goodness he got back when he did, in time to save the stupid boy's life. Luckily Sergeant Dewey arrived quickly. He helped Gifford carry Frank down to the shop, from where he was taken by ambulance to the Royal East Sussex Hospital.

Newly qualified house surgeon Dr Annie Ross[1] gave Frank heart stimulants and oxygen, but nothing the medical staff did could restore him to consciousness. At 2pm the next day he died, three months before his sixteenth birthday. The inquest was held at the town hall by Harry Davenport Jones. To assist the jury Police Sergeant Dewey produced a sketch to illustrate the loft and the trap door. Dr Ross gave the cause of death as asphyxia.

The 25th November was a sad day in Bembrook Road. Frank's neighbours congregated outside his home at no.119 to watch the funeral cortege leave. Frank was laid to rest in the Borough Cemetery.

Young Gifford went on to have a successful career in photography. It is a great shame that, because of a prank, Frank Smale missed out being a part of that. In 1952 Gifford advertised for two trainees, a boy and a girl aged about fifteen, to join the business. Doubtless he remembered with a tear in his eye an earlier fifteen-year-old he once knew, who threw away not only his career but his very life, just to play a joke on him.

Despite a painstaking search of the local papers between 1897 and 1907 (the decade surrounding 1902) I found no mention of anyone hanging themselves in any building in George Street.

1. Anne Ross was a twenty-eight-year-old Australian who came to the UK in 1920 and qualified in May 1937. After working as a hospital doctor she returned to her native land in 1950.

DIGRESSION: HARRY GIFFORD LEONARD BOYD

Gifford Boyd was born on 14th August 1917 at 4 Burdett Place, George Street, where his family lived well into the 1920s. His grandfather H.B. Boyd had been one of the pioneers of portrait photography in Hastings, with shops and studios at various locations. He left Hastings in 1904. Gifford's father, H.A. Boyd, ran a tea-room at 38 George Street and was briefly landlord of the Queen's Head in Ore, but in 1931 decided to follow his father's trade. He set up in business as a photographer at 3 Bexhill Road and opened a shop at 36–37 George Street, where in 1937 Frank Smale met with his fatal mishap.

Gifford, his mother Kathleen and his younger sister Kitty helped H.A in the business, and it was fortunate that they did, because when he walked out on them in 1939 (never to return) Kathleen took over and ran the Bexhill Road shop with Gifford and Kitty (a specialist in hand-colouring photographs).

In 1944 Kathleen died and Kitty married, but by then Gifford had his own shop, Boyd's Photo Stores, at 28 Castle Street. It had operated for a few months in 1939, but had to close whilst he was away on war service. He reopened at 36 Robertson Street in 1949, offering wedding and studio portraits, and also selling cameras, photographic supplies and binoculars.

The business remained in Robertson Street throughout the 1950s, whilst it flourished and expanded. He reopened branches in Castle Street and Bexhill, and placed three photo kiosks on the seafront and pier, staffed by retail assistants and photographers of both sexes armed with Leica cameras. He bought a pink, elephant-shaped seat which children would sit astride to have their photos taken. As increasing numbers of the public owned cameras he offered them developing, printing and enlargement services, and sold movie cameras and slide projectors. By the late 1950s he sold tape recorders and electric shavers. He gave film shows to children and old folk and awarded a yearly Gifford Boyd Cup for photography. In the days before mass television ownership he broadcast film footage of Princess Elizabeth's 1951 visit to Hastings in his shop window every evening.

From 1939 Gifford Boyd published photo-cards of Hastings scenes but few were printed, making them hard to find today. During the 1950s he started his 'Gifford Series' of photo-cards, mainly of Hastings, which included a set of six depicting the model village of Ganymede at White Rock Gardens, and one that shows Winston Churchill receiving his Golden Winkle from the Winkle Club in 1955.

His employees included Mrs and Mrs McPherson, parents of Madness frontman 'Suggs', and the father of Christine Keeler, the infamous model in the Profumo scandal.

After trading for fifty years, Gifford Boyd's Robertson Street shop closed in 1999. He died at Hastings in February 2004, aged eighty-three.

THE following appreciation of Mr. Grice appeared in Thursday's "Evening Standard":—

"The 'Evening Standard' regrets to announce the death of Mr. Edward Grice, for several years a valued member of the reporting staff.

"Mr. Grice was a versatile journalist, who, on many occasions, acted for the 'Evening Standard' as its special correspondent abroad. His excellent news sense and descriptive ability were shown in his distinguished messages from Palestine at the beginning of the troubles there. He was in the Saar during the Plebiscite. In Austria, after the Dollfuss murder, he did brilliant work in supplying his paper with the earliest news of the trial of the assassins, and the verdict.

"From a wide experience of crime reporting, he wrote the series of articles on the cases of the late advocate, Sir Henry Curtis Bennett, which appeared in these columns and were afterwards published as a book.

"Mr. Grice was a man of rare personal charm, generous and warmhearted. He is mourned in Fleet-street.

"He lost his wife in a tragic accident on Sunday last. Two young daughters are left."

HSLO 12 November 1938.
Corporal Teddy Grice aged 18,
Luton Times 2 July 1915.

The Wellington Hotel and its side
elevation on Castle Hill Road.

THE CORK CATASTROPHE

COLLINSWOOD DRIVE & WELLINGTON SQUARE

In 1936 the *HSLO* reported that Hastings had become a favourite weekend spot for numerous Fleet Street journalists, among them Edward 'Teddy' Grice of the *Evening Standard*. Eighteen months later he and his family moved from Hammersmith to 22 Collinswood Drive in west St Leonards. Teddy spent weekdays in London for work purposes, and so Eunice Jones, aged twenty-one, was engaged to help with the children and keep his wife company in the evenings.

Teddy, a station master's son, grew up on Luton station and became a rookie reporter on the local paper. After serving in a field ambulance unit of the RAMC during the war, he spent the 1920s as a crime reporter. His accounts of the notable trials involving an illustrious barrister were collected into a volume published in 1937 as *Great Cases of Sir Henry Curtis Bennett KC*. By then he was working as a European political correspondent for several London newspapers.

His wife, Sarah Hernan, was nine years his junior. She was raised on a farm in County Donegal along with at least nine siblings. Nothing is known of her adult life prior to their marriage in Islington in 1927, nor how she acquired the nickname 'Phil'.

On Saturday 5th November Teddy arrived home at 7.30pm. Phil, who was expecting a baby in two weeks, was in a cheerful mood after throwing a small, private fireworks party for their daughters, aged nine and six. The couple caught the bus to Hastings, where they visited a few nice pubs. Phil imbibed three or four whiskies and a couple of cocktails; she was merry, but not too inebriated to catch the bus home. After eating a snack whilst listening to the radio they retired to their separate bedrooms at about 11.30.

As soon as Teddy woke the next morning he smelled gas, which he quickly traced as coming from Phil's bedroom. He entered and threw open the windows. She appeared to be sleeping peacefully but he could not rouse her. Eunice went to fetch Edward Glynn, a young Irish GP, whilst Teddy and a neighbour tried to revive her. It was too late: she was dead, as was her unborn baby, and her pet cat, still stretched out on the bed as though in a contented feline slumber.

Dr Glynn estimated that Phil had died about 3am; after a post mortem he gave the cause as carbon monoxide poisoning.

Over the next two days Teddy received a series of nasty, accusatory anonymous letters relating to his wife's demise. The press did not reveal their exact contents. Another was handed to Coroner Harry Davenport Jones during the inquest on 8th November, after which he made some scathing remarks about people who sent such 'poison pen' letters. The culprit was never found.

At the inquest Teddy explained that he had effected a temporary fix in his wife's room by blocking the open end of a newly-laid gas pipe with a wine cork. When he entered her gas-filled room he spotted the cork lying eighteen inches from the pipe and quickly jammed it back in. In addition, a chair had been overturned, the electric light was on and a newspaper was on the bed. Sergeant Wills theorised that Phil knocked over the chair, climbed into bed and fell asleep reading the paper, not realising the chair fell onto and dislodged the cork. The coroner could not be absolutely certain beyond any doubt that it was an accident because there were other people in the bungalow who could have deliberately removed the cork. Remarking that the evidence 'troubled' him, he returned an open verdict.

The next day Teddy visited the Wellington Square Hotel to book rooms for himself and his parents before driving to Luton to bring them to Hastings for the funeral. He viewed three rooms on the top floor and paid a deposit to reserve them, remarking to a chambermaid and a passing workman that the rooms had lovely sea views.

A few minutes later the workman and his foreman were standing on Castle Hill Road looking up at the scaffolding when they saw Teddy standing precariously on the external window ledge of the rear room, smoking a cigarette. Ignoring their gestures to go inside he waved his hand before letting himself fall forward. He nosedived fifty-four feet before hitting the pavement. Someone raced across the square to no.45 and fetched Dr Delia Nesbitt Wood. She found Teddy spread-eagled on his front and beyond help. As acting police surgeon she conducted a post mortem herself; the cause of death was severe head injuries.

The inquest, under Harry Davenport Jones, returned a verdict of 'suicide while of unsound mind'. He remarked that Teddy's 'fortitude' might have held firm after the loss of his wife and child, but for the anonymous letters, the vile contents of which he declined to reveal. It seems that Teddy could not live with the guilt of what he had done by blocking a gas pipe with a cork. That he reserved three rooms and told his parents to expect him suggests that he did not visit the hotel in order to carry out a suicidal leap. It is likely that he had fought the urge to end his life for some days, and, looking through the window at the sheer drop he realised it offered an instantly-available way to terminate his unbearable anguish. It must have cast a powerful spell, because even knowing the additional pain his death would inflict on his already-motherless children failed to hold him back. He paused long enough to write four notes, which delayed his death for perhaps ten minutes.

When police examined the room they found the four sealed envelopes. One contained a note asking the police to inform his parents that he would not be collecting them and one was for the coroner, thanking him for the sympathetic way he dealt with his wife's inquest, adding: 'You were rightly puzzled, as I was, by the mystery.' The third letter was addressed to his parents; the last was to a friend. None threw any light on either his or Phil's death.

On Friday 11th November a requiem mass was held for Phil at the Roman Catholic church of St Thomas in Magdalen Road, whilst Teddy's Anglican committal service took place at St Ethelburga's. Teddy's family, a few neighbours and Harry Picton (who had built and sold them the bungalow) were joined by a dozen London newspapermen for the double interment at the Borough Cemetery. The two small children did not attend, but someone sent flowers on their behalf, bearing poignant cards reading 'To Mummie' and 'To Daddie'.

When the 1939 Register was compiled ten months later the bungalow was still uninhabited, and Eunice had moved next door as a companion to a pair of middle-aged spinsters. The children were in separate boarding schools not far from their grandparents' home in Luton.

The fate of Dorothy and Mary Grice

Their education complete, both girls married at age twenty-two; however, whilst Dorothy seems to have led a conventional, quiet and uneventful life, that of her elder sister Mary was an absolute train wreck.

The story of Mary's life is known because her husband, Jeffrey Bernard, wrote frankly about it in 'Low Life', his wry observational column in *The Spectator*, based on his life as a vodka-swilling Soho pub philosopher.[1] Using the name 'Anna', as a wild and promiscuous teen she had relieved him of his virginity on Hampstead Heath when he was fifteen. She was eighteen and already pregnant with a child that she gave up for adoption. Despite her sexual liaisons with his brother the pair married in 1951, though they later separated. Described as 'frighteningly volatile and unstable', Mary spent her twenties abusing alcohol and drugs. She attempted suicide four times, eventually succeeding in 1959 with a massive overdose of barbiturates. She was just twenty-nine.

It is hard not to conclude that the catastrophic course of Mary's tragically short life was influenced, if not caused, by the terrible ordeal she suffered at the age of just nine. Being three years older than her little sister, she doubtless was allowed to know more, and understood far more, about the deaths of her parents and her unborn sibling. Her demise brought the total to five lives (if one includes the cat) that were ended prematurely because Teddy stupidly stopped up a gas pipe with a wine cork.

References: *HSLO* 12 September 1936 & 12 November 1938; *Sunday Independent* 25 October 1992; *Daily Mirror* 10 November 1938 & 27 February 1959.

1. In 1989 his anecdotal ramblings became the subject of a long-running, award-winning West End comedy play: 'Jeffrey Bernard is Unwell', later made into a film and now on DVD.

Advert for the musical festival in which Philip's daughter played
one of the seven dwarves in 'Snow White' whilst he conducted his
strange experiments in the cellar of their home.

THE MIRROR MAN

CLOUDESLEY ROAD

There was nothing weird, strange, bizarre, eccentric or irregular about Philip King. His entire life, man and boy, was conventional; he was traditional, predictable, stereotypical and conservative. And yet his death was arguably the most bizarre in this book.

Born in Hastings in October 1909, his upbringing was absolutely unremarkable. His father was an upright and highly respected local businessman who served on the town council for decades. Raised in Silverhill and privately educated at King's Collegiate School in St Leonards, Philip played cricket for the South Saxons (becoming vice-captain of the second team), and founded Hastings Wanderers in 1932, becoming an accomplished bowler. As well as playing football for the YMCA and Hastings Observer clubs, he captained and coached the water polo team and was president of the Hastings Amateur Swimming Club, in which capacity he issued prizes and medals to the junior group, the Ducklings.

Having trained as a decorator and builder, Philip created his own successful building company, with offices at 122 Bohemia Road. One of his constructions was Our Lady's House in Carisbrooke Road, which Christ Church commissioned in 1952 as a home for eight aged and infirm parishioners. As a member of the Round Table he took a keen interest in its Halton Boys' Club; he was also an elected member of the Rotary Club and a Freemason in the Lodge of St Michael. He served on the executive of the Friends of the Buchanan Hospital and Friends of the Old People, chairing the latter's Collections Committee.

In both business and private life Philip was affable, reliable and wholly respectable. He was never involved in any wrongdoing, lawbreaking or anything remotely dodgy, and no whiff of scandal ever besmirched his good name.

At age twenty-four he had married Frances Thomas at a traditional white wedding at St Matthew's church, and the couple had two children. By his late forties he and his family enjoyed a typical middle-class lifestyle, residing in a semi-detached villa in leafy Cloudesley Road. He enjoyed good health and, even in middle age, doubtless because of his sporting activities, was a powerfully-built and exceptionally fit man.

Wednesday 12th March 1958 was the second day of the yearly Hastings Musical Festival, a competition which had been running since 1908. The King family's eleven-year-old was taking part with her classmates; she was playing one of the seven dwarves in a tableaux of scenes from 'Snow White'. Philip drove her and Frances to the White Rock Pavilion, then returned home. He had no work that afternoon other than a business appointment at 4.30pm.[1]

After the performance, mother and daughter made their way home. Frances found that she could not get her key to open the front door. Assuming it was a mechanical failure she rang the doorbell and, getting no response, rapped the knocker. Philip was definitely home because his car was parked outside, so she tried the bell and knocker again, this time more insistently, but to no avail. Luckily a ground floor window had been left slightly ajar and so she climbed in. As soon as she got inside the telephone rang: it was nearly 5pm and her husband had not turned up for his 4.30pm business appointment. His overcoat was hanging on its usual peg, so he could not be far away. Perhaps he was in the garden shed or had popped next door to speak to a neighbour. The house was cold and she wanted to light the living room fire; however, the coal scuttle was nearly empty so she carried it downstairs to the coal cellar to refill it. As she entered she saw her husband in the corner of the cellar, motionless, silent, and hanging by a noose.

Despite the terrible shock to her system Frances kept calm and did not panic. She hurried back upstairs for a sharp knife then quickly worked out where to cut the rope. He'd looped it around his waist, ankles and neck, so she sawed at the top part to loosen it from his throat as best she could. Philip was no lightweight and so she could not move him. She ran back upstairs and telephoned for help.

The first person on the spot was P.C. Clements, who attempted artificial respiration until Dr Gordon Nesbitt Wood arrived and said there was nothing anyone could do to revive him. The policeman examined the curious scene. Attached to the ceiling was a newly-inserted hook, and a 56lb weight was on the floor, attached to the rope. A block of wood was nearby, from which, he suspected, the deceased man had stepped off. There was a mirror facing the man, as though he had been watching himself.

At the inquest, poor Frances was so distraught she could hardly speak. When she did, she could barely be heard. Her personal grief in losing her husband so young was compounded by the inexplicable and shocking circumstances of his death, and to have the details exposed in an open court in front of friends, neighbours, strangers and reporters must have been the most excruciatingly embarrassing experience of her life. Her parents-in-law were in their eighties and intensely distressed and bewildered by their son's bizarre demise.

Dr Nesbitt Wood told the court that Philip was wrapped in a plastic mackintosh, which he had put on back to front and buttoned up to the neck. Death was due to asphyxiation from strangulation with a ligature. The coroner.

1. The whereabouts of their other daughter was never mentioned in the news reports. It seems likely that she was at boarding school.

Stephen L. Clarke, was baffled by Philip's actions; he asked whether it was 'within medical knowledge for persons to carry out experiments to see how far they can apply pressure to themselves'. The doctor replied that it was, adding that 'People think they will be able to control the pressure'. When questioned about the mackintosh he replied: 'One reads about people dressing themselves in rather peculiar ways and tying themselves up in these experiments'.

The coroner decided that there was insufficient evidence for suicide or accidental death, and decided upon an open verdict. In a brief news item the committee of FOTOP was clearly both devastated and mystified. The chairman said that Philip's death had 'robbed them of one of their finest workers' and had come as a 'great blow'. He appealed for someone to replace him in the organisation. At their last meeting Philip had been 'full of fun and full of ideas for the future, and apparently in the best of spirits.' Referring to the strange manner of his death he said, 'We shall know nothing of the illness which took him from us — because I am certain it was an illness — but we wish to remember him as he was.'

After a service at St Peter's, Philip King was buried at the Borough Cemetery. Rather aptly, the officiating clergyman was the Rev F.A. Mackintosh. Being widely known and respected in both his professional and his sporting activities, and having gained a large number of acquaintances from his work in clubs and charities, his funeral was exceptionally well attended, among them the photographer Gifford Boyd, who features in the chapter 'The Joker'.

A month later a fifteen-year-old schoolboy in Hampshire was found hanged under similar circumstances. The pathologist told the coroner that in his experience it was 'common for boys to perform such experiments on themselves'. There was another case just two weeks later and, browsing newspaper archives over the previous century, quite a number of accidental deaths of teenage boys arising from hanging or asphyxiating experiments.

Frances King never remarried. She raised her daughters with the help of close family nearby and continued to lead a very quiet and conventional life, dying at the remarkable age of 107.

References: *HSLO* 15 July 1933; 15 & 22 March and 3 April 1958; *West Sussex Gazette* 10 April 1958.

Infants found 'dropped' in Hastings 1859–1898

1859	on the beach	1883	in White Rock Road
1859	on the beach (another)	1884	in Chapel Park Road
1859	in Eft Pond, West Hill	1884	the beach at Pett
1859	in a well, rear of 7 Cross Street	1884	in a toilet at Warrior Gardens
1859	on the beach opposite Pelham Place	1885	in a garden at Hollington Park
1859	in a basket in a hedge in Deudney's field	1885	in a biscuit tin on the rocks at Caroline Place
1860	on a path above Tackleway	1886	on the beach at Bopeep
1863	behind a WC at Hastings station	1886	on the beach at Ecclesbourne
1863	in Newgate Wood	1888	on the West Hill
1863	In Magdalen Road	1889	at Hoad's Farm Wood
1864	in the WC on Mercer's Bank	1889	on the beach opposite Marina
1865	behind The Croft	1890	on beach opposite Eversfield Place
1866	in Mount Pleasant Road	1892	in Cambridge Gardens
1866	on Castle Rocks	1892	on Rock-a-Nore Beach
1866	in Stonefield Road	1892	by High Wickham
1870	in Gillsben Wood	1893	in a well behind the Royal Sussex Arms
1875	in Eft Pond, West Hill	1893	behind Magdalen Road
1876	in Sinnock Square	1893	in Wellington Square Gardens
1876	in a garden in All Saints' Street	1894	in Beaconsfield Road
1877	at Ladies' Parlour	1894	by the Rocket House, Bopeep
1877	at Bunker's Hill, Halton	1894	top of Wellington Road
1878	in a field at Bohemia	1896	on the beach at St Leonards
1878	on the beach	1897	in a hedge in Barley Lane
1880	in a lake in St Andrew's Gardens	1897	at Minnis Rock
1882	in St Helen's Wood	1897	in Alexandra Park
1882	at Laton Road	1898	on the beach opposite Marina
1882	at The Haven, Bopeep	1898	at Bohemia Farm

Fifteen Hastings women charged 1851–1898

1851	Hannah Moore	30	Concealment of birth. 2 years
1852	Sarah Judge	17	Wilful murder. No bill; discharged
1855	Sarah Head	28	Concealment of birth. Not guilty
1858	Emma Sutton	15	Concealment of birth. 6 months hard labour
1860	Caroline Martin	28	Concealment of birth. 4 years
1871	Mary Ann Downs	20	Concealment of birth. 18 months hard labour
1874	Lavinia Furner	19	Concealment of birth. 3 months
1874	Keturah Holter	36	Concealment of birth. 18 months with hard labour
1875	Sarah Lampard	n/a	Concealment of birth. Not guilty
1879	Alice Cardew	21	Concealment of birth. 1 month
1879	Catherine Dive	20	Concealment of birth. Not guilty
1880	Dora Penny	22	Concealment of birth. 3 months
1887	Annie Roper	19	Concealment of birth. Case dismissed
1891	Mary Good	18	Accidental death
1898	Mary Corbett	16	Concealment of birth. Not guilty

SPECIAL REPORT

A CENTURY OF INFANTICIDE

1799-1899

The most common category of homicide in nineteenth century Hastings (and indeed Britain) was the killing of unwanted babies by their unmarried mothers. In 1865 a correspondent to *The Times* described it as 'An evil which has steadily increased among us for years, and the proportions of which have at length assumed a character which it is impossible any longer to ignore'.[1]

Nobody knows, or can ever discover, how many infants were killed annually, because most were 'dropped', that is, abandoned in the hope that the mother would not be traced.

In Hastings an annual average of two were found, but in the worst year, 1859, there were six. Between 1866 and 1900 the deaths of seventy-three 'name unknown' newborns were registered. I found press reports of the inquests of fifty-three between 1859 and 1898 (see facing page). To this list must be added at least a dozen that were not found until years later: in the early 1900s there was a spate of builders and homeowners finding mummified bodies concealed in attics, under floorboards and behind walls, partitions and panels.

The mothers

When the mother of a 'dropped' baby was identified, she was invariably found to be a working class, single woman, and — as was every one in Hastings — a domestic servant. They were uneducated and, in most cases, mere teenagers.

Sex outside of marriage was considered immoral and bearing a 'bastard' child brought deep shame upon the woman. Girls were raised in state of ignorance barely imaginable today. Birth control advice amounted to being warned not to let a man 'have his way'. Rarely the instigators of sex, the typical pregnant servant was a naive girl who had been persuaded, seduced, tricked, cajoled or pressured, and sometimes forced, either by someone in her employer's household, or a man she was 'walking out with' (dating). As one man observed:

> That female nature — the instinct of attachment to someone of the other sex — has made them easy victims to being ruined...We all know that promises...are apt to deceive, where a woman trusts her good name to the truth of her seducer.[2]

1. 'LVH' in *The Times* 3 August 1865.
2. *Ibid.*

A brief one-off, encounter was all it took to set off a chain of events that so often led to complete ruin. Once pregnant, there was no way out. 'Certain people' would, for a price, 'get rid' of it, but the average teenager had no idea where to find them. Besides, the legal penalty was severe, and it was also a wicked crime against God.

About five per cent of births in Hastings were illegitimate, but not every one spelled disaster for the mother, especially in the country districts. Some married or cohabited with the baby's father; pregnant female servants with sympathetic parents might go home for their confinement, leave the baby with its grandmother and return to work. If she had (or the 'baby-daddy' provided) the funds, she might go away to another town, give birth there, then pay a woman about six months' wages to take it away and raise it (so-called 'baby farming').

The unfortunate girl or woman who had none of the above options and was dependent on her earnings would conceal her condition and carry on working, though it became harder with every passing month to conceal her ever-growing midriff. If found out she would be sacked and nobody else would employ her.

Openly having a child out of wedlock was impossible for the servant class. A 'fallen woman' elicited little or no sympathy. Charitable societies refused to assist them (because that would be 'rewarding immorality'). The workhouse would not take in a baby without its mother, but if she entered the dreaded place, then she could no longer earn a living and she would be stuck there indefinitely. So long as the baby lived, the unmarried servant faced being pitched into destitution or prostitution. Knowing these ghastly fates awaited her served to increase the pressure and the fear, and awakened in some a powerful urge to destroy the infant before it destroyed them.

Their sufferings can scarcely be imagined. They gave birth, alone and terrified, in privies, closets, basements and attics, trying not to make a sound despite the horrendous pain. Then, in the midst of fear and panic, they had to do 'something' with the unwanted newborn, especially if its cries might alert others to the fact of its existence.

The fathers

Reports of inquests, hearings or trials did not mention the person without whom there would be no baby. No woman named him; no attempt was made to identify him; no man came forward and owned up. All concerned held silence on the subject, as if they were bound by an unspoken agreement to allow the man to remain hidden and free from reprisals.

However, a trial that threw this bizarre state of affairs into sharp relief would sometimes provoke someone to break silence and fire off an angry letter to the press, railing against the anonymous man whose base urges were responsible for the girl's predicament. She had, in all probability, been seduced and — in the words of one (male) editor — 'ruined by the vile machinations of some libidinous scoundrel calling himself a man'.[3]

Educated women also began to speak out. In a letter to the *Hastings & St Leonards News* in 1860, prompted by the case of Caroline Martin,[4] an anonymous reader aired her views:

Neither in this case, nor in any of the undiscovered ones, have I heard the query '*Who is the father of the child?*' and yet this is a most important question; for I cannot believe that any woman would destroy her infant if she had the sympathy and support of its father. It is because he is a sneak and a coward — because *he* is so mean as to leave her to her trouble — so selfishly debauched as to care only for the gratification of his own passions — so cowardly as to shirk any part of the burden — it is because of this that such murders do take place; and therefore *whoever* the father of any such 'slaughtered innocent' may be he is not only a villain and coward but *accessory* to the murder; as *he* might have prevented it.

A striking contrast to this cowardice is the courage so constantly exhibited by [the] women. Without exposing or even naming those whose villainy has made them criminals — without trying to include them in the crime (though probably the crime has been *suggested* by the man) — without uttering a complaint against *them* — these women have borne the trial, the punishment, in silence.

It is an hypocritical mockery to talk severely of child-murder *while* the partner of the first crime goes unscathed. It is adding injustice to misery to punish *that* severely *until* society demands vigorously chastity in men as well as chastity in women.[5]

The editor of the *HSLO* commented on the subject in 1879, after two more were sent to trial. 'Where were the authors of the misfortunes of these wretched women?' he demanded. 'Perhaps sitting in your drawing room, making love to your daughter, in preparation for becoming your beloved son-in-law.' Such a man, he continued, 'murders with a smile and condemns [the woman] to public degradation and a criminal cell for a deed that was more his than hers'.[6]

---

3. *Standard* 20 July 1858.
4. Martin, a servant at 4 Carlisle Parade, pushed part of a steel crinoline hoop into her newborn baby's throat then hid the child in a box. Although found alive he later died. She was found guilty of wilful murder and sent to prison for four years.
5. *Hastings & St Leonards News* 4 April 1860. The italicisation was in the original.
6. *HSLO* 25 January 1879. In those days, 'making love' meant speaking of love, or kissing.

If the mother was identified, she would be delivered into the hands of men: doctors, policemen, gaolers, coroners, magistrates, public prosecutors, judges and jurymen. Only men investigated, judged and punished women; all female influence was excluded from the process. Women's role, as defendents or as spectators in the public gallery, was to wait passively to hear what men had decided and what punishment men were going to inflict on the woman for her wrongdoing.

Until 1800 the penalty for killing a newborn was generally execution, but over the years judges became increasingly reluctant to hang the culprit. An Act in 1803 created the lesser crime of 'concealment of birth'. This provided a means to reduce indictments from murder to concealment, for which judges could pass a light sentence of up to two years' imprisonment. The new Act heralded a general trend for all crime to be punished slightly more leniently, which arose from sentiments of humanitarianism that were beginning to gain traction at the time. There was also a growing awareness that the mothers were not evil but ordinary working women driven by desperation.

It was crucial, from a legal standpoint, to establish if the newborn had been stillborn or killed. The doctor conducting the post mortem would examine the lungs and decide whether the infant had breathed after birth. The verdicts of inquest juries rested upon his word, and he could save a woman from the gallows by deciding that her child was stillborn.

As the century progressed one can detect a subtle but discernible bias towards avoiding the conclusion that the newborn was deliberately killed. Coroners would nudge juries away from that verdict; some even ordered them to go away and reconsider if they reached the 'wrong' verdict. At one inquest in 1864 the Hastings coroner told the jury that if they opted for 'stillborn' they could wrap up proceedings immediately and everyone could go home. The jury duly obliged.

The Emma Sutton case of 1858 illustrates how much public attitudes had softened by mid-century. The fifteen-year-old daughter of a Hastings fisherman, Emma was kitchenmaid at an eating-house at 8 Robertson Street.[7] One lunchtime she gave birth in the water-closet, strangled the baby and tried to hide its corpse, but was caught by colleagues and handed over to the police.

The humane folk of Hastings raised a petition pleading for clemency on the grounds of her young age and because she lacked a mother to provide her with moral guidance. The judicial system allowed this terrified child to face trial for murder — for which she could have been sentenced to death — without any defence counsel. Fortunately, the jury found her guilty only of concealment of birth and she received six months in prison with hard labour.

7. Now part of Debenhams.

Not everyone agreed with this drift towards compassion. In 1865 the judiciary was accused of treating the mothers not just leniently but 'with the greatest indulgence'. The crime was 'fearfully on the increase', it was argued, and yet nobody seemed 'disposed to treat [it] with any real severity'.[8]

Between 1858 and 1860 eight newborns were dropped in Hastings, but only one mother was caught, prompting Superintendent William Glenister[9] to make the following irrational suggestion:

> If this most serious crime were more severely punished it would be of less frequent occurrence and I do not think that the sympathy of some (perhaps well-meaning) persons towards offenders of this class has a good effect upon those who are likely to commit such a crime.[10]

His advice was not heeded; in fact the opposite happened: sympathy and pity increased. Every time a Hastings woman was sent to Lewes Assizes on a charge of the wilful murder of her infant child, the indictment was reduced to concealment.

In 1874 there were two such cases. Lavinia Furner, the cook at 14 Markwick Terrace, and Keturah Holter, a servant at 2 Warrior Square, each strangled their newborn and hid the body. They were tried by different judges but defended by the same barrister, Mr Merrifield.[11] In Lavinia's case two doctors testified that the baby had been strangled with a strip of cloth. The coroner's jury duly returned a verdict that she 'of malice aforethought killed and murdered' her child. At the trial, however, her counsel Mr Merrifield cleverly argued that she had used the cloth purely to 'assist delivery' and had strangled the baby accidentally. The jury accepted this defence and, under guidance from the judge, found her guilty of concealment of birth. Keturah Holter admitted to strangling her baby, but Mr Merrifield argued that the jury could not be certain it had breathed.

It seems that age was taken into account when sentencing because Lavinia, nineteen, was given three months' imprisonment, whilst Keturah, who was thirty-five, received eighteen months — and with hard labour.

Only one letter published in the *HSLO* criticised the light sentence given to Lavinia Furner. The writer — 'Justice' — displayed considerable ignorance in asserting that these sort of crimes occurred because society failed to inflict sufficiently severe punishments on the girls who committed them. 'Justice' revealed that they had absolutely no comprehension of the cause of unwanted pregnancies, nor any awareness that infanticides happened back in the day when public execution and dissection was the deterrent and penalty.

8. SGO in *The Times* 5 August 1865.
9. Whom we met in 'Fishmonger's Folly'.
10. Hastings Annual Police Returns, October 1860.
11. Frederick Merrifield was a staunch and lifelong champion of women's rights. In 1872 he and his wife joined Henry Fawcett MP and his wife Millicent Garrett Fawcett to co-found the Brighton branch of the National Suffrage Society. His daughter Flora became a leading Brighton suffragist.

Between 1735 and 1799, eighty women were executed in England and Wales for the murder of their 'bastard'.[12] One of the last was teenager Elizabeth Lavender.

> On Sunday se'nnight the body of a new-born male infant, with its throat cut, was discovered, concealed in a small tub, among some cordwood, in a cellar at Fairlight. The fact appearing to have been recently committed, and suspicion falling on a young woman, resident in an adjoining apartment, named Lavender...The wretched girl hath scarcely attained her eighteenth year.[13]

On 21st January a coroner's jury found her guilty of murdering her baby by 'stabbing him in the gullet' with 'a knife of iron and steel'. She was incarcerated in Horsham Gaol for three months to await trial and on 25th March was conveyed to East Grinstead for the Spring Assizes. The main witness for the prosecution was too ill to travel, so Elizabeth was held in gaol for another three months until the Summer Assizes at Lewes in June. She was found guilty and sentenced by Lord Chief Justice Buller[14] to be publicly hanged four weeks later, on 15th July. It was surely a form of torture to leave a teenage girl to languish in gaol for six month knowing that her fate was to be publicly executed.

When the dreaded day arrived Elizabeth was conveyed in a cart to the gallows, where:

> Her behaviour...was such as became one in her unhappy situation. She trembled and wept much, but nevertheless seemed to listen to the Clergyman who attended her, and having expressed a hope that all other females would take warning by her untimely fate, she was turned off about half past twelve, and expired without any apparent agony.

The prison chaplain told the spectators, 'If ye have tears, prepare to shed them now.' The poor girl 'expired without any apparent agony', and her body was sent to be dissected and anatomized.

This ghastly tale has a nauseating twist. It transpired that Elizabeth's own father had ravished and impregnated her, and then forced her to pretend another man had sired the child. 'The depraved and unnatural father in now in gaol', explained the *Salisbury Journal*.

Elizabeth Lavender was the last woman in Sussex to be hanged for killing her newborn child.

12. More women were executed for this than for any other crime.
13. *True Briton* 2 August 1799.
14. Buller is (in)famous for allegedly issuing the judicial standard permitting a man to beat his wife with a rod, provided it was no thicker than his thumb. It's dubious whether he ever did so rule; nevertheless, he has ever since been lampooned as 'Judge Thumb'.

Thirty-year-old Hannah was housekeeper to the Rev Mr Abercromby Gordon and his family in a house that once adjoined the west side of St Andrew's Presbyterian Chapel, on the corner of West Hill Road and Boscobel Road.[15] In May 1851 Dr Gardiner gave Hannah some medicine for constipation. When she returned asking for 'something stronger', from her replies to his questions he ascertained that she was pregnant.

On 15th November, having somehow concealed her pregnancy from her employers and colleagues, Hannah went into labour at 3am. She rose at 6am as usual and performed her chores until 1pm, then went to her room, knelt on the floor alongside her bed, and gave birth. After cutting the cord with scissors she bound a cloth round the baby's mouth to stifle its cries and strangled it with four thicknesses of black thread. She tied a glass cloth round its neck, wrapped it in her lilac apron and then a duster and hid the resulting parcel in a box under her bed. She dropped the placenta into the water-closet and quietly returned to her normal daily duties. No one noticed any change in her demeanour.

About 3pm Jane Lamb, the chapel cleaner and pew-opener, found Hannah in bed. Seeing blood on the floor she remarked that she looked like 'a person who has had a miscarry or a child.' Hannah replied 'Oh dear me, nothing so bad as that, thank God.'

Mrs Lamb lived at 2 Victoria Passage (now Valentine's Passage), an alley connecting Shepherd Street with North Street. On 19th November Hannah secreted the parcelled baby under her red plaid cloak and walked to the alley. Asking a resident if she might use a privy,[16] she was directed to one in the back yard of 6 North Street. Late that night butcher James Pulford's teenage granddaughter saw something large and white in the privy. Her grandfather tried unsuccessfully to lift it out with laundry-tongs, then fetched Constable Barnes from his home at 9 Lavatoria. He tucked up his shirt sleeves, pulled it out with his bare hands and laid it on the Pulfords' kitchen table. Unwrapping the layers of fabric he revealed the corpse of a newborn boy.

By coincidence it was Mr Gardiner who certified the death. He told Barnes about Hannah's pregnancy, but when Barnes questioned her she denied it. After a placenta was found in the trap of the chapel's water-closet[17] she submitted to a medical examination by surgeons Mr Gardiner and Mr Frederick Ticehurst, to whom she confessed.

On Friday 28th November Coroner J.G. Shorter and his jury of eighteen men viewed the tiny body at Mercatoria Police Station, then convened at the South Saxon Hotel, 13 Grand Parade. Dr Gardiner's deposition was most damning: 'The

15. A block of flats covers the site.
16. A privy, also called an earth closet, was an outdoor toilet in a small shed. It had no plumbing and therefore could not be flushed. The contents were periodically collected and removed.
17. The chapel had a proper, plumbed toilet, known as a water closet, or W.C.

face of the child was black and the tongue slightly protruded. It had breathed, and its hands were clasped, evidently in agony. Death resulted from strangulation.' The jury retired for five minutes before the foreman, Charles Valentine Levett (a master baker living at 19 North Street) announced the only possible verdict: wilful murder.

Whilst awaiting trial Hannah was so ill that she was kept in the gaol infirmary. She told her nurse, Mary Ann Miller (of 8 Shepherd Street) that she had not intended to kill the baby, 'but by some irresistible impulse she couldn't help it'. At Lewes Assizes in March 1852 the jury found her guilty of murder, but recommended mercy. The judge ordered them to go away and reconsider. The men debated for a further fifty minutes and returned with a revised verdict of 'guilty of concealment of birth'. She was sentenced to two years' hard labour.

Hannah became pregnant in early 1851, whilst a live-in housemaid to the Duchess of St Albans at 5 Grand Parade. When the census was taken in June, three male servants were in residence, and research has revealed that the coachman, George Sims, had married Hannah six years earlier and yet both are shown as single. The censuses of 1871 onwards show them living together as husband and wife into their old age.

As a married woman, why did Hannah switch jobs, hide her pregnancy, and kill the child? Why did George allow her to suffer being publicly shamed as an unwed mother when in reality she was his wife? Why did he let her face a murder trial alone? The duchess may have sacked them for lying, but as a coachman George could have found a job elsewhere. It is perplexing.

* * *

Nowadays young women are no longer sexually ignorant. They are more streetwise and less easily tricked; contraception and abortion are legal and available, and unwed mothers are no longer shamed but helped by the state.

With the criminal justice system, levels of sympathy and leniency towards people who commit crimes are at an all-time high.
Teenage girls are no longer executed for infanticide, which became a separate legal category of offence in 1922. Nor do they serve long prison sentences for acts committed out of desperation. For example, at Winchester Crown Court in 2010, a girl of seventeen was convicted of stabbing her newborn with a knife and 'dropping' its dead body in a litter bin. She was given a twelve-month Community Supervision Order and a Youth Rehabilitation Order. A far cry from when Elizabeth Lavender was publicly hanged for the same crime.

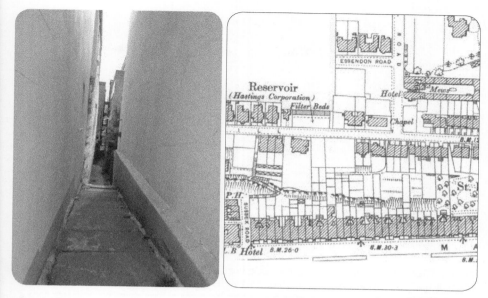

Victoria Passage, now called Valentine's Passage, in 2020. It still connects North Street with Shepherd Street.

Map: St Andrew's Chapel was situated on the corner of West Hill Road and Boscobel Road. Known in the 1830s as the 'Quadrangle Chapel', and in the 1860s as the 'Scotch Chapel', it was converted into dwellings which were later demolished. Modern flats now occupy the site.

A snippet from the 1851 census for 5 Grand Parade, showing Elizabeth Beauclerk, the Duchess of St Albans, her son, aged ten, who had inherited the dukedom, her daughter Lady Diana and her six residential servants, including house maid Hannah Moore and coachman George Sims.

Elizabeth Catharine Beauclerk	Head	Widow	47	Duchess of St Albans	
William Amelius Do	Son		10	Duke of St Albans	
Lady Diana Do	daur		8	Scholar at home	
Sarah Richards	Serv		40	Ladys maid	
Hannah Moore	"		30	House Maid	
Hannah Stolford	"		45	Cook	
George Sims	"		36	Coachman	
Thomas Mathews	"		26	Footman	
William Thackray	"		19	Under do	

The South Saxon Hotel, on the corner of London Road, was often used for inquests. It has since been rebuilt. It was no.13 Grand Parade, and no.5 was to the left, just out of the picture.

A MYSTERIOUS AFFAIR

An inquest was held touching the death of a male child, name unknown. Caroline White, the wife of William White, a boatman at the Queen's Hotel stade, and residing at 1 Bank's Cottages, said that on the Tuesday afternoon, about ten minutes past five, a man in the employ of the London, Brighton and South Coast Railway Company, delivered a brown paper parcel to her at her house. She had to pay tenpence carriage. The parcel had been sent from London. She opened it and inside found a little black bag. Inside this was a piece of very coarse wrapping containing the body of a child. The child was quite dead, and she had no idea who sent it. The parcel was addressed to Mr. W. White, 4 Bank's Cottages, Wellington Place, Hastings. The Whites had never lived at no.4 and no one by the name of White lived there.

Mr Charles Ashenden, surgeon, said the infant was three or four days old and was probably premature, as it weighed only four-and-a-half pounds. The railwayman who delivered the parcel to Mrs White said that it had arrived at Hastings station at three o'clock on a train from London Bridge. The railway company had no record of who sent it. The case was passed onto the Metropolitan Police.

Poor Mrs White had to pay tenpence for the dubious privilege of becoming involuntarily involved in the most bizarre incident of baby-dropping Hastings has ever seen. The police never solved the case. Paraphrased from the *HSLO* 27 September 1879. Bank's Cottages were behind 14 Wellington Place.

IF YOU ENJOYED THIS BOOK

Would you please rate it on Amazon? (You can review books on Amazon even if you did not buy them there.)

This really helps me, as a self-publishing author, to gain feedback on what my readers like.

Many thanks,

Helena

By the same author

Strange Exits from Hastings Volume One

Available at Albion Books (George Street), Book Busters (Queen's Road), The Bookkeeper (King's Road), Calneva (King's Road), Fishermen's Museum, Grand Designs (Grand Parade), Hare & Hawthorn (George Street), Hastings Museum, The Hastings Bookshop (Trinity Street), Sweet Selection (Robertson Street), 90 Norman Road, Turn the Tide (George Street), Waterstones (Priory Meadow), Ebay and Amazon.

Personally dedicated, signed and giftwrapped copies are available direct from the author via the website www.hastingspress.co.uk

STRANGE EXITS VOLUME ONE:
WHAT THE CRITICS SAY

"Thirty three deliciously dark tales of murder, misery and misfortune befalling Hastings residents and visitors...I read the book in one open-jawed, bug-eyed sitting...I absolutely bloody loved it" *Joel Griggs, owner, True Crime Museum*

"A factual, captivating, enthralling read." *Amazon reviewer*

"Well researched stories of macabre happenings around Hastings, from 1804 to 1948. Really interesting to find out more about the previous uses of buildings etc. Highly recommended book for Hastonians and visitors alike." *Amazon reviewer Paul W*

"Serious social history told in an entertaining, informative, and thought-provoking way. With the skill of a pathologist, the author peels back the skin on these deadly stories to reveal the human dramas behind the 'strange exits'.

There are also several unsolved murder cases where the author turns sleuth, cracking mysteries like a fearless and groundbreaking Victorian lady detective. Her unravelling of the Bopeep Railway Tunnel murder of 1891 is breathtakingly good, and one of the many highlights of this superb book." *Ripperologist magazine, June 2020*

"Researched with diligence and care...the stories are unique and intriguing. It would have been easy to sensationalise these seemingly far-fetched accounts, but there's a gentle humility, tenderness and even kindness in the way the stories are presented. I confess I inhaled it in just one sitting. The characters are so fascinating they tumble out of the pages and jostle for position in the forefront of your mind." *Elly Gibson, Hastings Independent Press*

"A gem of a book, full of detail and illustrated throughout with photos, maps and illustrations. A highly recommended read." *Amazon reviewer Stephanie*

"Brilliant and entertaining... a fantastically well-researched and beautifully-composed book, which will keep you enthralled to the very end." *Amazon reviewer Gary Feakin*

"Loved this book from the intriguing front cover to the many strange goings on in Hastings in days gone by. In a macabre way I just wish there were more stories as it was such an enjoyable read." *Amazon reviewer Frances Croton*

"Some of the tales are funny, some are gruesomely horrific, but all are intriguing and memorable." *Hastings Online Times*

"An absolute delight to read, so interesting and researched impeccably. To find out more of the dark history of my home town is both intriguing and thought provoking! Excellent!" *Amazon reviewer Kate*

"A fascinating dive into the darker side of Hastings. A compelling and addictive read. Highly recommended." *Amazon reviewer Paul Kennard*

"The author has gone into superb detail and her research has been flawless. A must for those who have a passion for local history and mystery!" *Amazon reviewer Steve Dadson*

"Written with an elegance and panache rare in the field of popular history... painstakingly researched, lavishly illustrated... A more compelling read I have not come across in a long while." *Amazon reviewer Eric*

"From the quirky, steam-punk style cover to the digressions, this book is full of delightful surprises...a collection of weird and outlandish ways that people were dispatched from Hastings into the afterlife." *Amazon reviewer Ray*

"Helena tells these stories with a researcher's eye for detail. She wastes no words and there are no fanciful passages, so every page is packed with detail. From the opening goat-attack (which gored a soldier through his scrotum) to gruesome deaths on the railway lines, it's a real gem of a book... a rattling little read and features some great photographs too, which allows comparison with our modern town." *Tony Harris*

"I couldn't put this book down. I read it in a weekend. Every story was fascinating, vividly painting gruesome tales with beautiful Hastings and St Leonards as the backdrop. Well worth a read if you are familiar with the area or have a taste for an unsolved mystery." *Amazon reviewer Veronica*

"This book has a local flavour but the stories are universal — they capture the frailties of human nature, the role of luck in so many of life's outcomes and the weirdness of which there is a little bit in all of us." *Amazon reviewer Craig Sams*

"A wonderful book, beautifully and painstakingly researched. Anyone who wishes a glimpse of life in St Leonards and Hastings in days past as well as the effectiveness of the criminal justice system should enjoy this amazing read." *Amazon reviewer Kim Hollis QC*

"Absolutely brilliant!, since this arrived in the post I haven't been able to put it down, packed with so much information and historical insights into people's lives, I have learnt so much." *Amazon reviewer Iain Hardwick*